Chasing Freedom

Chasing Freedom

Through the Word of Our Testimony, We Overcome

Sarah Grace Spann

ISBN: 1530491207
ISBN 13: 9781530491209
Library of Congress Control Number: 2016904132
CreateSpace Independent Publishing Platform
North Charleston, South Carolina

A Call to Remember

I used to become upset when my plans fell through; but now I see that it is God's protection from less than His best.

It was an ordinary morning. My alarm went off. I sat up in bed with my eyes still half closed, finally finding enough motivation to turn on the lights. I went to my closet and picked my outfit—nothing special, just the typical Nike running shorts and T-shirt. (I never have much drive to dress up for class.) I quickly put on a little makeup and then sat down with my delicious pumpkin-pie coffee. Even in summer, the aroma and taste of fall is one that simply comforts me and that I love. As I sat in my big brown comfy chair, I opened my Bible to start my quiet time with Jesus before class. Recently, I had been pursuing my passion for baking and cooking with every extra minute I had, and as I began my prayer to God that morning, part of it went something like this: "God, you have put this passion inside of me—along with my experiences with food serving both as an unhealthy and a healthy place in my life—for a reason. Lead me to what you want me to do with this passion of mine. Give me wisdom and insight as to where to go next…" I opened my Bible to Micah 6, as that was where my reading plan directed me for the day, and began to read. Right away, my eyes came to a halt at verse 5:

"My people, remember…Remember your journey." (Micah 6:5)

Any other day, I would have skipped right over that verse without giving it much thought. But today it meant something. Today, it meant something very significant. God opened my heart and eyes. As I began to reflect on my past, I realized what a challenging journey it had been. I had plunged into some of life's deepest valleys—experiencing great heartache, anger, fear, doubt, and other unexplainable emotions. However, during those tough times, I was also continually reminded of God's faithfulness and how far His love reaches out to us every single day. I was certainly refined by the fire more than I ever could have been without going through those valleys. Yes, He certainly turns all things into good. And, yes, He certainly turns ashes into beauty.

When I prayed that prayer that morning, I had in mind that I would write a cookbook full of delicious recipes that I loved creating. But, as always, God's ways are "higher than my ways" (Isaiah 55:9). I had felt before that I had life experiences to share, and I was beginning once again to feel God lay on my heart the need to record these events. Yes, I most definitely had a story to tell. I remembered it very well. And, this time, I would listen. I would listen, and I would share my journey.

I pray that God may move in your heart in unexplainable and unique ways depending on where life currently has you, as I take you on my journey. Come with me. Experience God's faithfulness and goodness as we both dive into depths of despair and climb to mountaintops of victory. Overcome your difficulties and become totally free as you come along for the ride.

Life is a Journey

*I used to think life was all about reaching the finish line; but now
I realize it's more about the journey there.*

FREE AS A bird. Yes, that was what I was growing up. Not a care or worry in my mind. Each day at sunrise, I would jump out of bed (already in my bathing suit because that was also my sleepwear of choice) and run around catching lizards. I would even hang them off my ear lobes.

My neighbors and I would play survivor all day in our lake, eating the weirdest of berries and leaves because "we were stranded" and making so-called clay pots out of the guck we would find. We would only come inside when called in for a delicious lunch of peanut butter and marshmallow fluff sandwiches. We would spend hours creating some ~~awesome~~ unique dances to Tarzan music, believing we were the best of jungle dancers. I had a rare talent of fake laughing so weirdly—not that we didn't already laugh enough from the ridiculous things we did—that all of us would break out in real laughter for hours on end.

As if all of that wasn't enough to fit in a day, I would even find some spare time to annoy my older brothers and sisters before the sun set. Yep, I was that annoying little sister who would cry to mom if I was shunned from hanging out with them and their friends. This was my everyday life—always beginning right as the sun rose so that I wouldn't miss out on a single minute of living life to the fullest, from the moment I got up until the last second of sunlight. I talked freely, I acted freely, I ate freely, I laughed freely, and I loved freely. Simply put, I lived freely.

When it came to the more important aspects of my childhood, I am thankful that I had a mother who raised me in the freeing love of Christ. From as young an age as I can remember, I recall waking up to my mom talking to herself in a soft whisper, or at least that is what I thought she was doing. I didn't realize until much later in life that what I heard every morning was actually my mother talking with God. To be honest, as a kid, I thought she had started to lose her mind a bit. However, waking up to her praying and falling asleep to her voice singing worship songs at night impacted my life in more ways than I realized. This intimate relationship with God was something she pursued each day, and it greatly influenced my spiritual walk. Her example sparked my initial desire for a personal relationship with God, and I chose to accept Christ when I was seven years old. I don't know where I would be today without her. And let me just give a disclaimer, she has had anything but an easy life. Still to this day, I have no idea how she did all that she did: raising three kids on her own while going back to nursing school to become a nurse anesthetist. She also somehow made time to wake up early enough to work out and make us breakfast every morning before waking us up, as well as making a home-cooked dinner every single night after a long day of work and taking us to sports practices. I may not have appreciated all that she did when I was younger, but I see now that she was a superwoman.

As I got older, I started becoming more indifferent to the way the world acted and less passionate about Jesus. Can anyone else who grew up in a Christian family relate? I think sometimes when you grow up surrounded with it all, it's hard not to get stuck in a rut of taking Jesus and all He did for granted, while slowly beginning to think that how the world acts around us is fine.

Throughout middle school, you could have referred to me as a "luke-warm Christian." I still believed in God and tried to do what was right. After all, that's what I had been taught to do all my life. I didn't curse, I didn't drink, and I didn't smoke or do drugs. I thought I was being a good Christian. But I never stood up for Jesus among others, and I kept more to myself when it came to my walk with God. I rarely talked about God except in Bible class when we had to because, well, I didn't want to offend anyone or make anyone feel uncomfortable. Thankfully, I did maintain a constant Christian sphere of influence, whether it was by my choice or not. With my Christian middle school and the family atmosphere through-out my earlier years, I never strayed too far away from the Christian truths I had been taught.

But then came my freshman year of high school. I felt as if I was gaining such a great amount of freedom. I was coming out of my little Christian bubble and going to a normal public school—a school where there was no set dress code or strict, excessive sets of rules about writing in cursive or praying before every class. I began meeting new people, and the way they lived and talked began to appeal to me more and more as I became closer to them. My new group of friends was anything but similar to my old group, and I found myself slowly accepting the mold I was be-ing pressured into. I wanted to fit in. I began laughing at dirty jokes that I didn't think were funny and gossiping about others, even though I knew I shouldn't be. Did you have that group of mean girls in your school? Yeah, I was a part of that group in my school for a little while. I would rather have been caught dead than to create awkward tension by mentioning my faith or asking someone to please stop talking the way they were. I kept thinking to myself, *Wow, I've been missing out. This is so freeing compared to my stifling little Christian school.* But what I thought was freedom was anything but that. Slowly, my indifference to the world's way of living—what I viewed as being freeing—actually began to take my freedom away, little by little.

And then all hell broke loose that year—my freshman year of high school—which is where my story really begins.

What happened that freshman year? "I know high school can be tough," some of you may be thinking, "but come on; I don't want to read a pity party." I promise you that this is anything but a book written to gain sympathy or out of sadness. Instead, it is a book to offer hope and freedom. Are you ready to take the journey with me, back through my past, in order to find freedom yourself?

Our journey together will travel into some very low places, places where sadness, anxiety, and trouble reside. But this journey surely does not end in the valley. After experiencing the darkness of the aches, pains, doubt, and despair, the light did come. By the grace of God, this journey has a finish line at the top of a mountain peak. This is not just the story of a period of my life. It is a journey of discovery: a journey to find happiness, hope, and—most importantly—to find freedom. Are you ready to embark on this journey with me?

The Landslide

— ∞ —

*I used to think having to eat my veggies was catastrophic. Now
I see that life comes with events that are much more devastating
than eating green beans or swallowing vitamins.*

MY PARENTS SPLIT up when I was a little girl—three years old, to be exact. I thought I was the luckiest girl. No, that is not a typo; I really did love it. Probably not right away, as I don't know if I even knew what was going on at the time. But when I got to be about 7 years old, my dad began bringing me over to our neighbor's house for dinners every once in awhile. She had two children of her own, and a cat that I loved chasing around the house trying to hold. I became close friends with this lady's daughter and son, catching tadpoles all day long and sailing them across the lake in our old yogurt containers. One day I remember even sitting in a circle on the grass by the lake with them, talking about how cool it would be if our parents got married. Well, shortly after they did. Little 7-year-old Sarah Grace walked down the aisle in her puffy, white, flower girl's dress excited for the new addition to the family. Now, I didn't have one, broken family, but two, loving families that I got to go back and forth between. My mom, sister Jamie, and brother Johnny were at one house; and my dad, stepmom, stepsister Anna, and stepbrother Eddie were at the other. I also had the privilege of getting to celebrate two birthdays, two Christmases, two Easters... you get the idea. Like most children, I loved celebrating holidays and I loved presents. *I love this double family life*, I remember thinking to myself. What child wouldn't see more presents as a good thing? I

5

gained a second mom, sister, and brother; and before I knew it, I felt so close to them. Of course, there was the typical fights any siblings have every once in awhile. But, that is exactly what we were, typical kids. A hairbrush thrown here and there, no big deal.

The bottom line was that I had a second family that I loved visiting and spending time with just as much as my other family. My dad let me have Pop-Tarts and ice cream every day, which was always a plus too. Life was good. My mom would have died a little inside if she had known what I was eating for breakfast over there. But all in all, I think the hardest thing I had to go through as a young girl was eating the yucky vegetables my mom always put on my plate before I was able to have dessert. Too bad we didn't get my yellow Labrador Dixie until *after* I began liking veggies.

As I grew older, though, things changed. Life became...well, hard. Things happened that I never thought would happen. And as a result, I began to feel helpless. Has your life ever seemed completely out of your control, with things happening left and right that you didn't expect and surely did not want to happen? Well, that is how I felt my freshman year.

As I entered high school, I was just beginning to not miss my older brother Johnny as much (who had left for college the year before), and then, my sister left. I remember being in 8th grade when Johnny left, and I cried for a week straight, sleeping in his bed every night of it. Even though he was much older than I, he was my hero – he could never do any wrong in my eyes. And he knew that, taking full advantage of it. Yes, even to the point of asking for frequent back scratches and fresh, hot grilled cheese sandwiches. Of course, I never thought twice and would come running at his beckon. Getting used to his absence was hard enough; and then my sister left the very next year. After being used to a house full of people and laughter and chaos, all of a sudden for the first time in my life, the house seemed empty. It was so quiet and very different with just my mom and me. Our house had always been filled with commotion—a house where, at any given moment, there were always tons of lively spirits, laughter, and activity creating an upbeat and fun environment. I remember coming home every day after being out with friends, to find all my brother's friends playing video games in the family room and my sister and her friends getting all done up—makeup, hair, and all—for their own personal photo shoots. (Yes, these occurred pretty frequently in our household.) Since I was a tomboy when I was younger, I usually went with the guys, playing 007 James Bond video games. When I got a little older and decided to begin acting like a girl, I wanted nothing more than for my sister and her friends to make me up and take photographs. Sporting red lipstick, curls in the hair, and a beautiful dress, I felt like a million dollars.

But my house that was once vibrant was now quiet and very lonely. While in high school, I came home to no one but my girl Dixie (our yellow Labrador). My mom worked late a lot of the time, so I would be alone in the house with no voices but my own. There was no one to hang out with, no one to dress me up and take pictures (okay, by now I may have had more mature desires), no one to simply talk to about my day or share what was going on in my life. I wasn't used to that; and I certainly did not like it.

Not only were my brother and sister gone, but when she was not working, my mom was often gone as well now that she had a serious boyfriend. In all my years growing up, she had never dated much at all. But now she had been with this one man for a couple of years that loved down the street from us.

They began dating when I was in middle school, and I didn't like it one bit—not because I had anything against the man, but it was weird to see my mom going out with someone. My mom was a special person to me (basically my best friend at the time), and I almost felt protective. I never wanted her to be with anyone but the best. At first my brother and sister attempted to keep me company and to keep my mind off of her absence. Thankfully, it worked and caused me to be indifferent to her relationship for a while. But then my brother and sister left, and the existence of my mom's relationship became a much greater deal to me. I felt more alone than ever. With him living only a few houses up from us in the neighborhood, she seemed to always be over there.

I was no longer spending my nights talking and eating dinner with my mom, brother, and sister; instead, I spent my evenings by myself. I would be lying if I said that this didn't create a slight bitterness inside me toward my mom's boyfriend, and it only got worse. See, it started to become very obvious how much he liked my mom, and how much he did not like me. What 15-year-old girl would take that lightly? I realized he acted nice most of the time, but that he was not very sincere in doing so. He had money, and he used it to his benefit. I felt like he was always buying things in order to win my mother's love.

Have you ever seen someone holding a baby, pretending to love it, but by the expression on their face, can obviously see how repulsed they are by the drool? Saying with words how cute the baby is, but in body expression, screaming with disgust. Well, that is how I felt around Bill...and I don't even have a drooling problem! Maybe that is not the best analogy, but it is a good portrait of the situation I'm trying to paint.

Bill was never mean or rude to me. In fact, he was always very complimentary when he saw me, saying how successful I was. However, his body language and actions verified what I had felt despite his words: I was just an annoyance, a barrier between him and my mom. The line of where I stood was thoroughly drawn when I overheard him telling my mom on the phone that he wanted to get married but only *after* I left for college. Okay, I wasn't perfect; I listened to their phone calls. (Throwback to the perks of having house phones.) But despite the fact that I was doing something I shouldn't have been, I was hurt. Part of me wished I hadn't heard what he said, but the other part was glad to know where I truly stood with him.

You can only imagine the strain this created on the relationship between my mom and me. I considered my mom to be one of my best friends, but she was torn between us. She didn't want to have to pick sides. I knew her heart and that she would always love family above anyone else, but I felt like she hated that I wasn't trying to get along with Bill. My mom took any comment of disapproval about their relationship personally, and my remarks only caused friction in my relationship with my mother.

I really couldn't blame her. Who wouldn't take it personally and wonder what was wrong with being together after dating a man for four years? Why wouldn't she expect me to try to make it work? But I saw something she didn't, something she couldn't see while she was in the middle of the relationship. Maybe I couldn't understand how she could be so blind at the time. But soon enough, I would be there myself. As you'll see, I too became blind to a part of my life that was toxic and secretly destroying me. But at this point in my life, I just wanted to be angry. I wanted to blame her for being so blind. And that is actually what I did, becoming full of anger and bitterness. As a result of my mom being the only family member still in the house with me, the environment became quite stuffy. Everything that I said that could possibly be taken in a negative way was taken negatively. And I would be lying if I said I was an angel through this time. All of my comments about how my mom and Bill shouldn't be together, combined with my disrespectful attitude, didn't help. I was certainly not perfect, and still am not; as you will see just how great my imperfection is as my journey continues.

These circumstances created negative feelings and emotions in my life. I was what you could call a "negative Nancy." (Poor Nancy, where did that saying come about anyway?) I was a typical high-school girl; even things that aren't a big deal, become a big deal when you're that age. Any little comment that could upset me or throw me into a rage, did.

But then I was blindsided by an event that turned my life upside down.

Remaining a Victim

I used to think the actual injury was what scared me; but now I realize it was the recovery process I feared most.

FLASHBACK TO THE summer before high school began.

I was keeping myself extremely busy with a new sport I had picked up: running. If you had known me before that summer, you would have wondered what girl I was talking about, because certainly Sarah Grace was not a runner. I played competitive soccer most of my life, and I even played point guard for the high-school basketball team in middle school (our school went from first-twelfth grade). But the required PE mile was the only time you would see me run for any length of time—any distance farther than that was a no-go. But when my close neighbor friends Katie and Courtney (who were great runners themselves) continued to encourage me to come out for summer training with the high-school cross-country team just to meet people, I reluctantly agreed. I remember saying, "Okay, okay, I'll come out and run. But I am only going to come out to stay in shape for soccer." Spoiler alert— ironically, you'll see that distance running eventually became my only sport.

I was going to bed quite early every night, as I somehow became accustomed to waking up at 6:00 a.m. every morning to run. How is beyond me, as throughout middle school you would never hear of me doing such a thing, especially on the weekends. But it explains why I didn't get the text message my phone received late one night until the next morning— a text message that radically changed my life.

I was still half asleep when my alarm rang the next morning. I looked at my phone to hit snooze and saw a text message from my stepsister. It read: "I just want to let you know, before you find out some other way, that your dad and my mom are getting a divorce. He was cheating on her. I'll call you soon to talk."

My body woke up instantaneously, even though it was the early hours of the morning. My heart sank. I didn't understand. How could this happen? Why? I was going to skip the running practice, but then I decided it would be a good way to get all of my feelings out. Throughout the run, I found myself replaying the message over and over again. My heart was broken over the fact that they were getting a divorce…a second divorce to have to go through. But then another feeling overwhelmed me: anger. I could almost feel the steam coming off of me as I continued my run. The morning sun's heat beat down on my body, and my anger welled up as tears began forming. I was so angry at my dad for doing such a thing. I was angry at the fact that he was one of the greatest Christian influences in all of our lives, and now, well, that picture of Christ was completely fogged up. This meant no more "going to Dad's" and hanging out with my whole family that I had known and loved since kindergarten. I felt bitter toward my dad, who had hurt the people closest to me and torn our family apart. I was so angry inside that I decided to cut off all communication with him.

I had a few dinners here and there with my dad after some time had passed, but while I would try to be civil, things never felt the same. And, honestly, I didn't want for things to ever feel the same with him again. He had hurt not only me but also the people closest to me in ways I didn't think he would ever understand.

Was this the reaction I should have had? The right thing to do? Not even close. But I was hurt. And, unfortunately, I let the hurt get the best of me. I let the pain I was experiencing dictate my actions. I have come to realize that I was choosing to remain a victim at this point. See, it was much, *much* easier to say, "poor me" than to go through the recovery process and find healing in my relationship with my father. The healing process is often much more painful than the actual event itself. I was choosing to remain in my sadness instead of rising as a victor by engaging in the painful recovery process. I was living as a victim because of what others had done *to me* instead of living as a victor because of what my God has done *for me*. Unfortunately, that's not the first time I chose to remain a victim, nor would it be the last.

Have you ever felt at a loss for words to describe your feelings and emotions? Have you ever held on to bitterness toward someone who has hurt you—even though that choice ended up hurting you the most in the long run? Have you ever felt like your whole world was turned upside down by an incident or what seemed like a landslide of events? Like you have completely lost control over all circumstances in your life? Can you relate to the idea of running to other things when you are not able to have what you want? Turning to something that you never thought you would after hitting an all-time low? Do either of these responses sound familiar?

You are not alone. I was there. If you feel like there are chains right now in your life weighing you down, I promise you, there is hope. Freedom did not come right away for me. Becoming a victor instead of a victim was not instant. It was a process. It was only after many attempts to run from my problems, to run from my pain, to run to other resources, and to pull the "poor me" card that I finally saw the truth. You can become a victor too. Let's continue on this journey to find the hope, the happiness, and the freedom that you have been longing for.

Desiring Control

*I used to find peace and comfort through having control; but now
I realize that the greatest gift I have been given is the freedom of
knowing there is Someone better in control.*

I WAS A total wreck. For a girl who always had everything under control, everything in order, everything planned out...for once, I didn't have the answers I desired. I had lost all control of my life, or at least that is how it felt. Everything that I thought was sure in life was suddenly in chaos. Or, even worse, it was gone. I couldn't take it. I would fall asleep crying at night because I didn't know how to fix the emptiness and feelings of helplessness.

Every aspect of my life that I had taken for granted, was no longer the same: the quietness in my house with no siblings present...my mom's boyfriend who didn't truly want me in his life...my family being split apart for the second time...losing my father-daughter relationship. The worst part about it all was that I had no control over any of the things that were happening. I couldn't be my own solution anymore. I had been a perfectionist who thought she could fix it all, and I had to realize that I couldn't fix any of it.

There was a simple solution to finding peace during this time. There was someone who was in control...someone who I should have been more than thankful to have in control of my life. But instead, I craved to take matters in my hands. Instead of turning to my faith to change this desire, change my perspective, and—most importantly—give me peace and hope, I chose to fight to gain some type of control myself.

In our darkest days and in our deepest struggles, we do have a hope that we can turn to: The One who *is* in control. His name is Jesus. By His death and His rising from the grave, we have complete freedom. We have already been delivered; we have been set free. Any circumstance that we go through, He knows. He is in control, and He is constantly offering us comfort, hope, and peace to get us through.

Unfortunately, at this point of my life, I decided to settle for wandering around on my own, like a lost sheep. I continued struggling to overcome obstacles and find peace my own way, instead of living in the freedom—the promised land—that I had already been given.

The result was anything but good. It led to turning to something that I never thought I would…something that would take over my mind, my next few years of life, and ultimately, my freedom. And once I went down that road, it was not an easy one to turn back from.

Finding My Source of Control

I used to think I was invincible from certain things; but now I realize that belief only leads to being overtaken from those exact same things.

I ATE ANYTHING but healthy food growing up: "typical junk-food lover" would be a good description of me. Let's take a look at how I ate on a typical day just for fun: Toaster strudels, waffles with chocolate syrup and peanut butter, and Pop-Tarts were my breakfast foods of choice. For lunch, well, I was a picky one. Peanut butter (and only peanut butter, hold the jelly, please) on bread was my favorite sandwich—except when I could sneak in marshmallow fluff too. The only other option I found acceptable was turkey and butter on bread. Dinner was when picky Sarah Grace really showed her colors. My mom would make a huge, nice, healthy chicken dinner with vegetables, but I would have none of it. I would stick my nose in the air and ask for mac 'n' cheese instead—or I would order Chinese takeout. Don't even get me started on veggies. Those little guys were nonexistent in my diet. The only type of green thing you would see me putting in my mouth was green apple-flavored candy. Vitamins? No thank you. I distinctly remember every morning I would come down for breakfast, as a kid, and my mom would give me my daily vitamins. I also distinctly remember that every morning (always right after getting those vitamins) I would politely ask if I could go outside to check the weather "so that I could see what I should wear." By the way, I lived in southwest Florida where it was never anything but eighty-eight degrees.

At least the plants were well nourished. (No, she never caught on.)

So there you have it. I was a kid who ate everything and anything I wanted. Throughout middle school, I would laugh at all of the girls around me trying dieting methods: When you're hungry, eat saltine crackers, and drinks lots of water. Don't eat carbs. Skip breakfast. Don't eat past 7:00 p.m.

I found it all so ridiculous and hilarious at the same time. I thought, *I would never want to do any of that. I could never do such things. I love food way too much.* I lived as free as a bird, in all areas.

But little did I know what I laughed and joked about then would soon take over my life.

As I said, my freshman year of high school, I craved control. And food was one area I could control. But by the end of my freshman year, I was way too thin. My weight had severely dropped. I most certainly did not plan to lose weight—or even want to—but I did. Since my weight loss was gradual, I truly didn't realize what was going on at first. It took a while to become noticeable, both to me and to anyone else.

Losing a significant amount of weight after already being a naturally thin girl was not my plan. At first, I blamed my weight loss on the causes not in my control. Some excuses had truth in them—others, not so much. I had started taking antibiotics my dermatologist had prescribed, and the pills had caused me to lose my appetite for a while. After noticing about a five-pound weight loss, my mother had me stop taking them. But the weight never returned, and the numbers on the scale continued to decrease. I kept telling my mom and friends that I wanted to put the weight back on because I thought I looked terrible. That was not true. It could not have been more opposite of my current mind-set actually.

Did the pills cause all my weight loss? They may have originally sparked the ability to control how much I ate. I mean, I was a lover of food, after all. And I'm not sure if I could have restricted my food intake through self-denial alone. But then that hurdle was cleared because of the pills' side effects. Looking back, though, I realize the pills were not the driving force or the root of my problem.

I turned to food as my source of control. It's crazy how things happen without a person meaning for them to happen. I didn't think to myself, *What can I turn to for control? Oh, food! Yes, I will turn to food for my sense of control in life.*

But, subconsciously, I began thinking to myself, *Well, if I can't control any other aspect of my life, I'll control the food that I eat...*or don't eat. Unfortunately, what I thought would give me control really only took away the little control I had left. I would fill myself up on anything and everything that was low in calories, making sure I *controlled* my calorie intake. I still had the huge appetite that I had always had once I got off of the antibiotics, so I satisfied my hunger pains with meticulously created meals made up of any food that had almost no calories. I ate broccoli and watermelon all day long. I would count every single calorie that entered my mouth. Not one swallow of food went by that I didn't add into the "total allowance" in my head that I had set up for myself that given day. If I didn't know the calories exactly, I would estimate—always way overestimating the calories that I actually consumed.

It became a game to me to see how little I could eat in a day. I began spending hours and hours looking up nutritional facts. *Peanut butter has how many calories? Oh wow, no more peanut butter for Sarah Grace. Oil is high in fat? No dressing on salads anymore.* Avocados, nuts, fruits like bananas and mangos, all fell into the same category. Basically, any healthy food that provided good fuel for my body was out the door. And any kind of bread or high-carb food like potatoes, well, that was nonexistent in my diet. I became fearful of eating out, since I wasn't able to control the calories in the food. Any time a friend wanted to go out to get our typical Moe's burrito or Cold Stone Creamery ice cream that I use to so freely eat and without a second thought, I quickly made up an excuse as to why I could not go. Way too many calories for me.

I lost relationships as I began to isolate myself. Food began dictating every aspect of my life. It even took away the joys that were still present in my life up to that point. I no longer hung out with friends much, as I couldn't predict the food they would want me to eat during the time spent with them. My close friend Katie and I use to have ice cream together almost every single night. Now, I would have none. I might have Greek yogurt with a few chocolate chips on a good day – and still I would eat the last bite in guilt because of eating later than I had "planned" (therefore, was not in control anymore).

And then there was running. Running was something I had come to love. It was my outlet. But I was pulled out of running early in my sophomore year because of my low weight. My mom and doctor she had been making me go to frequently made the joint decision, and I had animosity toward both of them because of it. I remember it clear as day. I went to cross country camp with my team like we did every year, making a road trip to North Carolina to spend a week of torturous double day runs in the mountains. Except this year was different from freshman year's camp. I was no longer letting myself eat all the extra food my body needed to recover and maintain weight. While the other girls were snacking on cookies and s'mores at night, I would eat a protein bar. The result? I came back home to the scale reading ninety-five pounds. On a five-foot-six-inches girl, that weight not only looked terrible, but was dangerous. The frightening part looking back though, was that I thought I looked good. Yes, I would appease the doctor and my mom, telling them I knew I looked bad and that I wanted to gain weight. However, secretly I thought I looked amazing. I even posted swimsuit photos on social media (which now disgust me looking back).

I was in denial; but everyone else around me saw the problem clearly. My weight was the elephant in the room that no one wanted to talk about. Well, except my mom. She clearly wanted to talk about it. But I would have none of it. Every day when I went home, she would say things like, "Sarah Grace, you're destroying your body! You look terrible! You're killing yourself!" I would make up excuse after excuse as to why the weight had disappeared, which convinced everyone for a while. But when the weight never returned after some time had passed, the fact that I had a problem quickly became apparent.

I was under the false impression that if I could gain any sort of control, I would feel okay again. What do you look to for security? Does having your doors locked make you feel secure? Having a ton of money saved up? A high GPA? A great career? A lot of friends? Your outward beauty? Your own strength? Even though I didn't realize it at the time, I had turned to food as my security. Little did I know that food would give me neither control nor security. In fact, my newfound "diet" was destroying what I had left. Even though I actually consumed very little food, preoccupation with food began taking up all of my time, all of my thoughts. My mind was constantly on food.

I wish I had known then what I've come to learn now. Nahum 1:7 says, "The Lord is good, a refuge in times of trouble. He cares for those who trust in Him".

The Lord is good. Let that resonate inside of you for a minute.
He is a refuge in times of trouble. Let that sink in.

Food couldn't give me that peace that I was so helplessly seeking. Food failed me. It never satisfied that pit inside of me. It didn't fill that emptiness

that all of the unfortunate events in my life had created. My food obses-
sion only drove me deeper and deeper into a destructive valley: the valley of anorexia. Sadly, I was convinced I would find fulfillment in all the
wrong places. And as you can guess, those places failed me.

But as God has clearly shown me now, only He can give me true
peace. It's an unexplainable peace. One that you can have no matter how
dark the day or week seems to be. He is the only one that will neither fade
nor fail us. God's peace is a beautiful thing, but it is also hard to grasp
when we have no other example of it that is close in comparison. Think
about it: every other person in our lives will ultimately let us down at one
time or another. Even those who love us most. Every single thing we think
will lead to happiness or security fails us at one point or another. Or the
excitement of it quickly fades. But God offers a sense of fulfillment that
never fades, a peace that is unexplainable, and a love undeniable.

Whatever you may be attempting to find refuge in, I hope that you
will learn what I finally came to discover and still work on reminding myself daily: God is my security. Food certainly couldn't satisfy my need. It
couldn't help me. It couldn't comfort me. And it certainly couldn't love
me. No matter what we turn to for security, nothing on earth—no dead
bolt on your door, level of achievement, number on the scale, beauty,
career, academic accomplishments, or personal relationships—can ever
offer us a sense of security that will never fail.

The good news is this: God can give us that security. And He is already offering it freely. He loves us before we even take our first breath,
and even while we are running away from Him, He pursues us. God's love
gives us ultimate security because His is a love that will never fade, will
never disappoint, and will never fail us. To me, that truth is mind-blowing.

Two Are Better than One

I used to love the idea of being completely independent; but now I realize dependency is key.

As my sophomore year progressed, my state of health progressed as well; although it certainly was not for the right reasons. I wasn't truly healed on the inside. Mentally, I still struggled every day. I still feared eating unhealthy food, and I was constantly preoccupied with thoughts of food. I even began having self confidence issues that I had never experienced before; I no longer believed I was beautiful. This was new. Unlike some instances when an eating disorder comes from feelings of low self-esteem, the reverse happened in my situation. Struggling with my disorder created feelings of ugliness and insecurity that I had never felt before. I finally came to reality that I was only skin and bones as I looked in the mirror. I watched my beautiful, once-voluminous hair, fall out. I continued to push friends away as I began to completely forget the fun, carefree girl I used to be. I forgot what it was like to not plan what I would eat in a day. I forgot what it was like to spontaneously go out for ice cream with a friend. I forgot what it felt like to be free. I felt hopeless; which only made me want to control my food more. But I wanted to run again, and the only way I could do that was to put on some weight. So I did just that. And sure enough, my dietitian gave the okay to begin running again after gaining some healthy weight.

Slowly over time, I did begin to heal in some ways. I didn't feel the need to use food as a control tool as much anymore. And day by day I strived to become indifferent to the troubling events in my past. But the root of all my problems, the state of my heart and mind, was still not completely healed. I remained chained down to my past, unable to find the freedom I so longed for.

Things may have looked like they were getting better from the outside, but they were far from perfect. I hadn't reestablished a relationship with my father. My mother was still with Bill. But now things weren't as bright and sunny as they once had been between the two of them. Unfortunately, this was the year the economy—along with the real-estate business—took a turn for the worse. And Bill, who was a well-off real-estate agent, was slowly falling into a period of depression.

My mom has always had a kind heart and desire to help others, so she tried to remain in Bill's life to help him find his joy once again. But this, of course, created a larger barrier in my relationship with my mom. Now I didn't only disapprove of Bill for the reasons mentioned earlier, but also because I watched my mother's happiness diminish as she tried to help him. She was continually giving but never being filled, and she was eventually running off empty. Like all of my other problems, I just tried to pretend it wasn't happening.

As I look back now, I am reminded of the great need for community and accountability in life. The Bible says things like "two are better than one" (Ecclesiastes 4:9) for a reason. It is so important not only to pour into people's lives but to be filled back up by others too. It's key in life to have people who hold you up when you're struggling, encourage you to become better, support you in the dark times, and hold you accountable to the goals and values you've set for yourself. The results of having community and accountability versus not having it could be seen in my mom's situation. My mom was continuously pouring herself out without being filled, and I saw someone who was slowly losing all happiness and energy. On the other side though, I am thankful that I had my mom for accountability. I was able to keep my head above the waters in my time of struggle instead of completely drowning. I would have never made it out of this valley without her. Two are surely better than one.

But as I said, I was running again—but not just physically. I was running from all my problems as well. Was that the solution? The healthy answer? A long-term fix? Not at all. Was that what God desired me to do? Certainly not. But I was just beginning to get back up again from being knocked down, and I was nowhere near stable on my feet again.

And very soon I would take another hit...a hit that took me a long time to recover from.

Hope Comes in the Morning

I always told others to find hope in God through their darkest days; but I didn't realize how hard it was to do until I had to take my own advice.

MY HEART DROPPED as I saw flashing lights and a crowd of people outside a big, empty house the night of April 15. As I pulled into my driveway, only a few houses away from the scene, my mom unsteadily walked down our driveway toward me, and fateful words I had never dreamed of came out of her trembling mouth: "He's dead." Filled with panic and confusion, I had no idea what to do next. I started to bawl and to wonder how this could happen to anyone, let alone a man who had been so important to my mother. This heartbreaking event hit a very deep place inside of me.
Let me rewind.

Earlier that year as a sophomore in high school, Bill had told my mom he would try to reach out to me more. He had invited my mom and me to dinner, and he had told us earlier that day he would come over at 5:00 p.m. to pick us up, since we only lived a few houses away from him. I remember running around trying to get ready after a long day of school and a tough cross-country practice, as Bill was usually always right on time.

I was surprised when 5:15 p.m. came around, and we had yet to hear my dog bark—our signal that someone was at the door. Around 5:30

p.m., my mom and I figured we better walk down to his house, thinking he must have either lost track of time or that he was busy doing something that we could help him with. We walked up his driveway to the tiny black code box on the side of the garage. We knew the code; it was the way we had entered for years now. We punched in the four digits, pressed the key button, and up came the garage door. That was all a series of predictable events; however, what came next was anything but expected. The rising garage door unveiled a scene that made my heart pound at a pace quicker than it had ever beaten before.

As the garage door rose up, my mom and I were overcome with car-engine fumes. I felt like my heart instantly dropped deep into my stomach—usually only something I experienced when jumping off the high dive or when riding a roller coaster. We looked at each other and both of our complexions were white. I began to tremble, unwilling to go any farther inside. The nurse in my mom rose up, and she went running into the garage. Frantically, she began looking all around the garage and inside of the car—engine still running—for him.

He wasn't there. She ran up the steps to the garage entrance of his house. Taking a deep breath, she opened the door and found him lying right inside, unconscious. Hysterically, she sprinted to the neighbor's house for help and called 911.

The ambulance arrived just as Bill began to come to again. He soon regained consciousness, and after some medical checkups and attention, he seemed to be fully recovered. I was relieved Bill was okay, but I began to feel very confused in the days that followed as I observed him. He acted like nothing had happened. One day he had almost lost his life; yet, the next day he acted like it was any other day. However, that scare—that feeling in my stomach, that pounding of my heart—was not easily forgotten.

We were certainly more aware of his physical and mental state after that day. My mom worried about him every day, carrying the weight of his emotional well-being on her shoulders. I realized he needed support more than ever in this season of his life, and we began doing more things together, as a family would. We had dinners together every night and went to church together every Sunday. He even began talking about what room would be mine in his house one day. And, somehow, I was okay with it all. But there was one thing I realized as I began spending more time with Bill: just like I had turned to food for a sense of control and fulfillment, his security was most likely found in his money. And with the economy at its lowest in years, that was a dangerous place to find it.

We thought that Bill was experiencing more hope in his life, and then the dreadful night of April 15 came.

Fast forward back to where this chapter began.

As I came home late one night after youth group with Katie and Courtney, I passed ambulances and fire trucks in Bill's driveway and was then greeted by my mom, who was shaking intensely as she walked down the driveway to me. I had to face the hard reality that Bill had decided to end his life that night.

My mind and heart were filled with more emotions and feelings than one girl should ever feel in one night: sorrow, confusion, heartbreak, pity, uncertainty, weakness, anxiety, hopelessness, discouragement, and defeat just to name a few. I realized that I needed to look forward, focus on myself, and come to terms with his death, rebuilding the brokenness that this event had caused in my life. But my heart also broke for both my mom and for him. My mom felt as if she had failed in her mission to give him hope. And she had just lost the man she had loved for the past five years. And Bill...well, he had felt like he had nothing to live for. He wasn't able to find any worth in himself. With the turn of the economy, his confidence and hope went down the path of lies that Satan loves us to believe, and he allowed Satan to convince him that he had no reason to live anymore.

Throughout my life, there have been many things that I have looked to for security. Outward beauty, weight, athletic ability, academic success...the list goes on. However, every single one of those things have let me down at one time or another. I have come to realize that Bill's tendency to find security in his money was no different.

Unfortunately, this world is filled with lots of things that tempt us daily as sources of comfort and confidence. Even though there is nothing wrong with most of those things if enjoyed in the right amount and context, there's a major problem when we elevate any of these things too highly in our lives. It's like having idols back in the olden days. We may not worship golden statues like some people did in Old Testament days, but our misplaced focus certainly leads to the same result God tells us to avoid: making any *thing* higher than Him in our life.

Bill's situation was an example of what I struggle with every day too. His despair exemplified the truth that when we depend on anything else in this world, it will fail us and ultimately lead to destruction. Jesus is the only true satisfaction and foundation for a confidence and security that will never fail. Unfortunately, his story didn't end with believing in that truth.

Because of this tragic event in my life, I also began to believe some of the lies again that Satan often places in our minds: the lie that I was worthless, that nothing in life was good, and that life was screwed up beyond any hope of recovering. Satan's greatest lie began to seem a little more believable to me at that time in my life: the lie that God is not a faithful or a good God.

Have you suffered a terrible defeat or an aching experience in life? Are you allowing the lies that Satan loves to feed us to penetrate your heart? Are you beginning to consider his lies as truth? Please do not give into the lies like Bill and I did.

No matter how much loss my mom and I felt that night, God never left our side. He never does leave our side. He was there that night, and that truth became clear in my life the very next day.

An Unforgettable Night on the Track

I used to think feeling God's presence was only something that happened in the ancient days; but now I realize I'm capable of feeling that same, incredible strength myself today.

Bzzzzzz. MY ALARM sounded at 5:45 a.m. the morning after Bill passed away. It seemed like only an hour had passed since the horrific scene I had witnessed the night before, but the alarm indicated otherwise. Sleep had refused to give me even one wink of itself that night. But as tough as it was, I knew I had to get up and attempt to go to school. I had a track meet later in the day, and as a captain I could not let my team down. That is my personality in a nutshell. I always feel the need to be strong and in control—or at least come across to everyone else that way. I successfully made it through classes until lunch; it was a huge blur to be honest. I'm not sure what I looked like physically, but I know I felt as empty as a ghost on the inside. People passed me right and left in the hallway, some even bumping into me to get past. None of them knew the story behind the blonde, skinny girl they had just passed. Maybe they were thinking of the assignment due next period they hadn't finished. Maybe they were thinking of what they'd get for lunch. Maybe they were thinking of what they would say to that cute guy next to them in the class they were headed to. But one thing is for sure, they were not thinking about the tragic event I had just experienced the night before and how it was affecting me. Even most of my closest friends would pass me that day completely oblivious. My current state and story remained unknown to all. That day, I felt unknown to all. But then the wall finally broke down as I walked into Coach Kelly's back room, and I poured out my feelings to her and my close friend Katie. "Go home, Sarah Grace," I remember them telling me. "Get some rest. You don't always have to be so strong." I listened reluctantly and went home.

That afternoon I was not able to sleep or to eat a single thing. This time for once, it wasn't out of restriction, but out of complete despair and anxiety. And when the time for the meet approached later that night, no one expected me to attend—except the officials with the list of racers' names. But, deep down inside, I felt this unexplainable need to go. I felt called to run the two-mile race. I knew people would think I was crazy with it being less than twenty-four hours after his death, but I followed my gut. Everyone on the team had heard about the tragedy of the night before by now, and I questioned how I would handle seeing my teammates. *Please, just don't say anything or ask if I'm okay*, I thought to myself as I got out of my car at the track. As I walked over to my team, I saw faces full of compassion. *Be strong, Sarah Grace*, I repeated over and over to myself. I couldn't break down again. The looks of sympathy I was receiving left and right were more than I could handle. Sympathy was not something I ever searched for or desired. I was strong. I was independent. I didn't need anyone. I could handle it. Well, at least that is what I tried to tell myself.

I put on my racing flats and walked over to the starting line of the two-mile race I was registered to run. I shook my head as thoughts began to flood my mind: *Coming to this meet was a mistake. I can't run. I haven't slept or eaten almost anything at all.* And then a still, small voice spoke in my heart. Even though I hadn't been walking extremely close with God lately, I knew it was Him as I heard, "Yes, you can do this. Run with *my* strength. On your own you may not be able to run tonight, but with Me, all things are possible." Goose bumps spread over my skin, and I whispered, "God, I know I have absolutely no strength, but yes, through you all things are possible. If anything comes out of this race, I know it is you and you alone."

Bang! The gun sounded, and off I sprinted. I ran those 8 laps with all my heart until I crossed the finish line—in first place. The joy I felt was unexplainable. It was not the simple joy of winning I had known before. It was a joy of experiencing something very incredible, something supernatural. My teammates ran over to me with arms wide open and began to celebrate my feat with big smiles and loud shouts. *God, You are so real and You are here with me,* I thought to myself as tears came to my eyes.

How Often I Forget

The act of forgetting comes so naturally; but I realize that to have faith in the hard times, I must daily remember His goodness in my past. It is remembering that frames my perspective for what He will do in my future.

THAT IS NOT the last time I saw God's strength, power, and incredible goodness. But at that moment in my life, it became evident to me, as never before, how real God was. As I said earlier, I had grown up in a Christian home, and my mom was an example who truly shined Christ's love and the truth of His word, but I still lived indifferently. Yes, I went to church every Sunday morning—Sunday school too, of course. I even went to youth group on Wednesday nights. From the outside, it may have looked like I couldn't have been closer to Christ. You would have thought Jesus and I were besties. But little did I know what it truly meant to be a true follower of Christ. It wasn't until much later that I realized it wasn't about attending church or not doing bad things. It was about having my very own personal love relationship with the Lord Himself—a relationship where I spent time reading His word, talking to Him on my own time, and simply walking through all of life's daily events together.

A new spark of hope came into my life one day when my mom shared a verse with me from Habakkuk. Many days she would call me over to her to hear a verse she wanted to read to me or to recite a verse when it applied to a situation. But this time, it planted a seed deep in my heart. Habakkuk 2:2 says, "Then the LORD replied: 'Write down the revelation and make it plain on tablets so that a herald may run with it'" (NIV).

My mom went on to tell me that I should be specific in what I ask of God—that I should truly think about what I would want Him to do in my future and then write it down. (Kind of like a vision board, which I have become a big fan of recently.) I wasted no time typing four things on a Word document that day, and I saved it under the title, "Sarah Grace's Desires." This was the list:

1. Complete healing of anorexia: internal, external, and in my relationships
2. A best friend: with whom I can walk and grow with in Christ
3. A guy: who will truly love me for who I am, has eyes for no one else, loves Christ above all things, and who will also help me to grow
4. A state-championship title in cross-country in 2009

I saved that document, but soon afterward I let it escape my mind.

It is easy to forget things—including spiritual lessons and truths. The night after winning my memorable race was one of the first times in my life I had truly experienced God's power and presence. Was that the first time He was present? Certainly not. He was always there. But my eyes were finally beginning to see; I was finally starting to *get it*—to feel His presence when I talked to Him.

Unfortunately, my revelation of God's faithfulness slowly began to fade from my memory. I got busy and distracted with all the little things on my daily to-do list. And I slowly began resorting back to my old ways of living my life. I began feeling down about all the destruction in my life—whether it was within my family or within my own body. I also began experiencing some situations with friends that caused me to become angry—whether justifiably or not. I began wallowing in my misery and having a pity party for myself, making everyone else the bad guy. *I didn't deserve this all to happen to me. Why was I having to go through this all. Why didn't God protect Bill from coming into our life, or stop my dad for hurting me, or prevent me from falling into this eating disorder I just couldn't seem to fully shake?*

I could sense my need for control igniting within me once again.

My enemy of the past slowly crept back into my life. Once again, I knew that food was one area in my life that I could find that control. Food was always what I focused on when I wanted to pretend none of the other things in my life were happening. When I didn't know what else to turn to, food was my answer—or at least the focus on food was. My weight began dropping again. But this time, I was frustrated with the whole cycle. I began to question everything I had begun to believe. *I thought God had healed me from this. Why am I finding myself struggling again? Is God taking back his healing on my life? Is God bringing this destructive lifestyle upon me again? It's so embarrassing to have others see me struggling again.* So many thoughts flooded my mind.

I have come to learn that it certainly was not God "taking back his healing" or anything remotely close to that. We all have our weaknesses. We all have temptations that are harder to resist than others. We all have things we know are not healthy for our life, but for one reason or another, are attracted to them anyway. We all have something we tend to run to in order to cope with our imperfect lives. For me, hyperfocusing on food (which just happen to lead down the path of an eating disorder) was one of my greatest weaknesses.

And when I wasn't walking close to Christ, living in *His strength* and not my own, I was going to open the doors for my weaknesses to come back into my life again.

Idols Exist in More Forms than Golden Statues

I used to think you had to put something above all else in life to get to the top; but now I realize how destructive that belief is.

THE SUMMER AFTER my sophomore year flew by, and my junior year came quickly. My weight continued to waver back and forth constantly, and I had good and no- so-good months. But I always seemed to stay at a good enough weight to avoid conflict with my nutritionist or my mom. I convinced myself I was healed, but at that point I did not even realize the true meaning of being healed. Neither my heart nor my mind were in a healthy place.

From the days of "I'm only running to stay in shape for soccer" to the present, things had changed. I began taking running very seriously, pouring all my energy and time into it.

What did I love about running? I would get that question almost every day. Who would want to run miles upon miles for fun? But I loved the friendships; how can you not become close to someone you're running side by side with for an hour every day? Katie and I, even though close since becoming neighbors so long ago, spent hours upon hours together just on runs each week together with our coach, Kelly, talking about any and everything. I also loved the feelings of accomplishment after completing a workout I never thought I would; I felt like I was on top of the world.

But when it came to the actual act of running miles in the ninety-degree Florida weather, I can't say it was my favorite. Nevertheless, I was always a competitive girl, so even when I didn't necessarily love something completely, I wanted to be the best. Yes, I was always the one in middle school getting enthusiastic about exam review games and getting frustrated when someone on my team didn't know the answer. And the same goes for P.E. kickball games.

I've always said my dedicated, competitive, perfectionistic attitude is one of my best and worst qualities. It has given me the drive to do what I do and accomplish what I have. But it has also led to some negative outcomes.

Why had I started running? It was because two of my close friends, Katie and Courtney. When I moved to a new house in the second grade, I instantly became the best of friends with the two girls who lived next door. One was a year older and the other a year younger; we quickly became inseparable. We played from sunup to sundown, playing survivor, picking berries, swimming in our lakes, making delicious treats, creating trampoline routines, playing otters in my pool, and making up those infamous dances to Tarzan music. You name it, and we probably did it. This was Katie and Courtney.

These girls had grown up as runners and had run for fun and competed since middle school. They (unsuccessfully) attempted many times to get me to go out for the middle-school team, but I nicely turned down the offer. But remember how I was nervous to go to the huge public high school after being in a small Christian school my whole life? Their persuasive argument that summer training would help me make friends succeeded. And when I finally began training with the team in high school, I had been surprised that, over time, running became one of my favorite hobbies—even in the days when I could not run a couple loops around the local community college. I had definitely started at the bottom of the totem pole.

However, Katie and Courtney, as all athletes are, were also competitive. And when running became elevated to an unhealthy position in my life my junior year, problems soon developed.

I began putting running above all else in life and relying completely on *my strength.* That combination would never result in anything positive. But it made sense to me. Running was something I was good at, something that was a talent, something I had natural ability in. I felt independent, strong, and competent when I was running. Sadly, those last few statements exemplify how focused I was on myself. I believed fully in my own abilities, and it showed.

Wanting to be the best, relying on only my own strength, and placing running above anything else...all of those added up to a recipe for disaster. And it didn't take long to see that.

Being Number One Isn't Everything

I used to think I had to be first to be seen as successful; but now I see that mentality ruins a lot of great things in life.

I WAS ENTERING my junior year of high school, and running had become everything to me. Our team had some incredible summer training, Katie and I were both in the best shape we had ever been in. We had natural talent, but our coach was able to bring that talent to a level of fitness we had never achieved before. Coach Kelly knew what she was doing. We completely trusted her, and she found the perfect balance of never overtraining us but always pushing our limits to the max. The number of workouts when I remember saying, "Kelly, I can't go another mile...I can't do another four hundred" are countless. Yet, somehow, I always finished. She knew how to bring out a side of us that made us want to push ourselves to limits we didn't think existed. Katie and I noticed that our running times were significantly decreasing from the past couple years, and we couldn't be more excited about it. We had worked so hard all summer, pushing each other day in and day out, and we both knew that year's possibilities were endless.

Unfortunately, as our times decreased, we began not only treating every race like a competition, but also every practice like one; we both wanted to be the best. Well, let me speak for myself, I wanted to be the best. And even though I didn't intentionally take the competition to a personal level—a level that would get in the way of our incredible friend-ship—I did. Tension rose. Our teammates could sense a stiffness in our interactions at every practice. Looking back, I have only myself to blame, as I definitely fed the fire. I began to take every comment of hers and overanalyze it, making it seem like she was out to get me in my head. Of course, this only led to secret bitterness and making passive aggressive comments here and there.

As we lined up to start each repeat during our workouts, my mind was set on finishing first. The year hadn't started that way, but things quickly changed as the season progressed. At first we ran *with* each other, push-ing ourselves to our fullest potential. We were simply two girls giving our all. But somewhere along the line, that healthy competition was lost, and our close friendship vanished with it. Actually, our friendship hadn't been quite the same since I began struggling with anorexia at the end of my freshman year. As I mentioned, I lost a lot of friendships in that time of my life, and this was one of the ones that most certainly suffered. Why? Because she believed in confronting situations and talking about them. And I wanted no part in such a thing at the time. Instead, I pushed every-one away, including her. But we had slowly left it to a place of simply not being close friends anymore. Now, we had crossed a line to a place filled with unhealthy competition, tension, and bitter feelings.

Looking back, it breaks my heart to see what competition can do. What it *did* do. There is healthy competition—the dynamic that makes you want to become your best and strive to grow every day. Then, there is unhealthy competition, when the focus becomes fixated on comparing yourself to oth-ers and beating or becoming better than others. That's when problems de-velop. Katie and I went from being best friends to not even talking, from carpooling every day to barely saying more than five words when we saw each other in our driveways, from hanging out every moment we could, to only spending time together when we absolutely had to at practice. Our coach finally sat us down saying, "It doesn't matter what kind of relationship you have off the track; when you are at practice, you are captains; and you need to work together for the team's sake." And from there on out, that is exactly what we did.

But as the season went on, things only got worse. Teammates began somewhat taking sides, and it was clearly evident to anyone who knew us that we were no longer close. I remember one workout when I could feel the tension as we sprinted off, repeat after repeat. We were no longer racing against the stopwatch to beat our best times; we were only racing against each other, hoping to finish first. It was terrible. Well, again, this is how *I felt* and where my heart was at the time at least.

The conference meet came around, and then districts, and then regionals. We both did amazingly well at all three, placing one and two each race. We used each other to push ourselves to our fullest capability. The state meet was looking great for both of us, and our rankings continued to increase after each meet. We tried to act like things were okay between us, but the gap in our relationship was growing wider. From the outside, you may not have even noticed. But when the practices and races ended, so did our communication. We drove the same roads home and walked up driveways within steps of each other, yet, we did it separately.

The state cross-country race came up quickly, and we were both ranked within the top five runners in the state. I had gone from finishing essentially unranked my freshman year, to securing nineteenth my sophomore year (even despite the months of being pulled out because of weight), to now possibly being in the top five. The two weeks leading up to the race, I couldn't think of anything except for the famous grass horse track in Dade City we would soon be stepping foot on for the third time. This was the location every year for the state cross country race in Florida. So from here on out, everything I ate, everything I drank, and everything I did, I did with purpose to be ready for States.

I vividly remember the night before the race when we sat in my coach's hotel room. She was so excited for my teammate and me, yet she cautioned us both because of the difficulties in our relationship with each other throughout the season. She asked us to stay after the team meeting after excusing the rest of the team. Then she sat us down on that uncomfortable hotel bed, and with a serious look on her face, she proceeded to say, "You two have two choices: you can come out number one and two in the state tomorrow if you run to your greatest capability and work together as a team, *or* you can settle to compete only against each other and not even make the podium. It's your choice."

We nodded and agreed to work together. Unfortunately, we said one thing with our mouths and decided another in our hearts, whether consciously or not.

(Katie and I leading our team to the start line)

Bang! The gun went off, and we all darted out of our starting positions. The state course was on a grass horse track, and the finish line was on top of a slowly rising uphill stretch—a slowly increasing hill that runners had to conquer three times throughout the race. Somewhere around halfway through that 5K race, I fell off the leading pack of runners, getting discouraged and giving up mentally even before the last mile. Oh, the power of the mind. A little later, Katie fell off the lead pack. Our race unveiled the truth, even though we would never say it. We had chosen the latter of my coach's options, but the race was not yet over.

The first eighteen minutes flew by, and we were now approaching the finish line. Katie and I were now around sixth and eighth place, and heading up that last uphill stretch. I could see her clearly, just yards ahead of me. All of a sudden, I saw her waver back and forth, catching herself on the side fence that ran around the inside of the horse track. *Oh my goodness, what's happening to her?!* I thought to myself. She staggered again, but this time she dropped to the ground. I now was approaching her, unable to do anything. I so badly wanted to help her despite our long season of personal competition, but couldn't. I may have wanted to beat her that day, but I surely didn't want this to be happening or the way I did it.

You may be wondering, *Did you actually feel that way? Did you actually hurt inside as you passed her?* And the answer is yes; things change fast when someone's health is at risk. You realize, despite any tension or bitterness in the past, just how much someone means to you when something like this happens. Quickly my focus of the race changed, and all I cared about was knowing that she was okay and seeing her cross that finish line. Yet, I knew the rules: I couldn't touch another runner. I proceeded to finish the race and immediately turned back toward the last stretch where runners were sprinting towards me now. Sprinting past her now. I got on my knees. I called out encouragement to her. My heart broke as I saw her slowly stumbling to the finish line, as yet another runner flew by her, knocking her down to the ground again as they brushed past. I sat there unable to do a thing. My coach was in a similar position, knowing she could not help Katie either until she crossed the line. All the bystander's hearts were breaking as they had to watch this terrible misfortune occur right in front of them. She slowly crept across the finish line, instantaneously being swept up by the paramedics and taken to the ambulance.

Thankfully, she ended up being okay. The paramedics ran some different tests on her, and nothing too severe was wrong. With some rehydration and recovery time, she would be back to her normal self. But, needless to say, neither of us finished in the top five as had been predicted earlier that morning. No, neither of us stood on the podium that day.

I began crying uncontrollably on the way home that day. I was so distraught at the outcome. How could *I* have let this happen? I thought *I* had control over everything, and that everything was going to go just perfectly according to *my* plans. This was going to be *my* year to shine. What happened to the way things were supposed to go?

Do you see a pattern in my thinking here? I learned a couple huge lessons that day.

First, I simply could not place running that high in my life. When putting anything too high in your life, it can become bad – even if it is a "good" thing. Running and having a certain level of competitiveness in itself isn't bad. But for me to elevate running to such a high place in my life, that I was depending on myself instead of Jesus, and becoming so competitive that I placed winning above things of true importance like Katie and I's friendship, it began serving a negative role at that time in my life.

Which leads me to my second lesson of that day: I should never have let competition ruin such a wonderful friendship. Years and years of friendship filled with wonderful memories and times of compassion and care, became momentarily absent from my mind because of seeing her as competition and misinterpreting many of her words and actions. It just goes to show how placing something too high in your life, letting it become an idol, isn't going to end well.

Third, I learned I could not rely on myself. I could not rely on my own strength. After all, it was my own strength that had failed me. Both Katie and I's strength that day had failed us. And even though you may be successful for a short time like we were, it will never hold you up for long. God's strength is and will always be the only thing that will not fail us, whether it be in our athletic competitions or any other aspect of life.

I think the greatest lesson I took away from the whole experience though was to never focus on being number one. See, I used to think that success meant being number one. I used to think that my goal should always be to come out on top. But it was that exact thinking that led me to the terrible outcome that state race. The goal to be number one had led to losing a valuable friendship, missing out on God's best for my life, not reaching my potential, and—most importantly—ruining my testimony I could have had as a team captain.

But like many lessons we learn in life, I did not accept any of these truths or live by these lessons right away. Even though sobbing all the way home from that race, I didn't walk away from it realizing I needed a change of heart. Actually, the complete opposite happened. I started Christmas break of my junior year in complete disregard for anything that I knew was right. *If things weren't going to go well and according to my plan when I was doing all the "right things" according to my long held Christian values, then why continue to do the right things?* This was the thought that went through my mind upon getting back from that state race. And boy is that a dangerous one.

The New Sarah Grace

*I used to think becoming "like everyone else" would be freeing
and fun; but now I realize that "fun" lifestyle is actually very
suffocating.*

I'M JUST GOING to live life and have fun for once, I thought. I believe the
acronym YOLO would be an accurate depiction of this period in my life.

"You only live once" (aka YOLO, for my mother reading this out there),
was certainly my mentality going into Christmas break of my junior
year. After the horrible end to the cross-country season, I decided I
just wanted to have fun. I had never really been one to drink much or
go to parties like most of my friend group in high school. As much as
I would like to say it was because I knew God desired me to stay away
from those things, that was not my main reason. I knew that partying
and drinking wouldn't allow me to be the best athlete or student, and
I wanted to be the best at everything. So, along with the braces I had
worn for the last 3 years, I also rid myself of all my inhibitions and values during that Christmas break.

I was a "new Sarah Grace." That's what the guys told my friends at
least. And I loved it. I loved the new attention I was getting from everyone, especially the guys. Before Christmas break my habit was to be
asleep by midnight, at the latest, and to be up to run by 6:00 a.m. But that
wasn't the case anymore. Almost every night that Christmas break, I went
out with my new friends, and I began to mold into a person no one, not
even me, ever thought I'd be.

Along with a new group of friends and a different lifestyle, came a new boy—one among many who I had recently spent time with. I knew he was just showing interest as a guy wanting to have a fun time – nothing more, no commitment. But that didn't bother me for some reason even though it normally would have. I mean, wasn't it "fun" that I wanted as well?

Now I know what you are probably thinking to yourself when you read the words "no commitment" and "fun" in the paragraph above, so let me talk about something I'm sure you all are wondering. There was one rule I had promised to stay true to a long time before, and even though I was currently nowhere close to Christ, I stayed true to that promise. It was a promise I made years before – to remain sexually pure. I'm not completely sure why, but that was the only value—from all the values and standards I once had for myself—that stuck with me during this "yolo" season.

My new lifestyle continued into the spring semester—partying, having fun, and doing everything I could to tune out the convictions inside my head. Prom was just one night of many where the details are a bit fuzzy. But I was having fun, right? Plus, track season was actually going surprising well. Who would have thought that living this type of lifestyle wouldn't totally sabotage my running ability? *Hmm, maybe this isn't a bad lifestyle after all*, I thought.

During this time the little voice inside of me remained—the one that always seems to give us a small nudge here and there about the right thing to do. This voice was telling me very clearly that this life I was living wasn't right. At first, it spoke very loudly inside of me, making me feel a substantial amount of guilt. But slowly, the more I denied it and continued in my ways, the less I heard it. The deeper I went into that lifestyle, the softer the voice became. The sad part was, I was living an unsatisfying, unfulfilling life…yet for some reason I felt stuck in my choices. I would end most days feeling so empty and unhappy, yet continue to live the next day identical to the last. I was stuck. Can you relate at all?

I never thought there was any hurt in going waist deep into the ocean of worldly fun, but slowly—to my surprise—the tide took me farther from the shore than I could see and deeper than I could touch. I finally came to the point where I wanted out of my partying lifestyle. I wanted to live a life that brought true satisfaction and joy, not just a temporary high. I was being suffocated by my new way of living—the same lifestyle that was supposed to be freeing and fun. I thought I was only going waist deep, but I was swept out much farther than intended by the tide. I was slowly drowning.

But, thankfully, I have a lifeguard that walks on water. We all do.

God had a way of getting to me just in time. He seems to have His way of doing that. And He always has a master plan. No matter how much we may screw up or how far we may run, The Shepherd always comes searching for His lost, misled sheep – sometimes in mysterious ways.

During my junior year, a sweet girl sat behind me in my math class. Her name was Emily. I hadn't been close with her before that year, even though we had some of the same classes in the past. But, since we sat together in this class, we began talking occasionally and found ourselves bonding over our shared misery. The professor was anything but sweet, and the class was anything but interesting.

Every third period I would watch this smiling girl with bright-blue eyes saying hello to everyone. Not with the typical, I feel like I need to say it, hello. No, there was something different about this girl. She radiated with an authentic joy. She didn't have to say that she cared about every single person she came into contact with, because it was revealed in the way she treated them. She never failed to ask me how my day was, always waiting for and genuinely desiring a real answer, not just a "good". One thing I began realizing was that in most of those math classes, she would begin talking about her church and youth group. Not in an annoying way like you may have experienced with someone in your life. Simply just little comments here and there when appropriate in conversation. She rarely ended a conversation with me without failing to mention how she wanted me to come with her to youth group one Wednesday. I would respond politely, and consistently, each time: "Yeah, that sounds cool; I'll come sometime."

I really never had any intention of going. I went to church every Sunday with my mom, but only because I had to. I walked in and out of the same church doors without any thought of changing how I was living. It was just a routine; something I had to check off my to-do list.

I continued to make excuse after excuse as to why I couldn't go to church with Emily. We would text back and forth a little, mostly questions we had about that terrible class. But then she began to send me texts late at night with verses and things God had been teaching her, and I didn't know what to do with them all. First I was confused as to why she would send them so late at night, then I realized that was when she did the "quiet time" she always told me about—the time she set aside to read her Bible and journal. One thing about all of those late night texts, was the joy and hope they shined with. It wasn't just her texts that radiated happiness either; it was Emily's every word and expression. Like I said, I had never seen someone so happy or genuinely sweet to every person she came into contact with. I remember appreciating that about her a lot, and still do. It's not every day you come across someone who is truly genuine and not just putting on a smile to get something in return. But that didn't change my decision of not going to church with her. Still, I made excuse after excuse. I may not have been happy, but I also wasn't ready to turn from my ways.

I specifically remember one night I was at a party with my friends. My phone vibrated in my pocket, and I took it out and squinted at the screen. My vision was blurry, and I had to put all my energy into trying to comprehend what it said—especially with the chaos of people having fun all around me. Who would have guessed. It was a text from Emily, with a Bible verse. *Not even reading this one*, I thought to myself. I put my phone back away, afraid that I would feel bad about what I was currently doing. Receiving a text from Emily while at a party was not just a one-time event. It was a frequent occurrence. And it continued to occur more and more regularly as time went on. I have to admit, I found these interrupting texts quite humorous after a while, as I continued living my life of fun.

Yes, I was still choosing to run from the truth: Running away from what I really needed to deal with. Running away from the pain. Running toward what I thought would fill that empty void. The partying, the boys, and the "fun life" continued to be my lifestyle up through most of the summer before my senior year.

Isn't that why we turn to things that offer us only momentary pleasure? We believe the lie that these things will actually satisfy us and bring us lasting joy? We believe that void we've been feeling deep down inside will finally be filled? Or maybe it's that we've got sick of waiting. Waiting for healing, waiting for that opportunity to come up, waiting for that person that has hurt us to apologize, waiting for that family member to break from their addiction. Instead of continuing to wait, in hope of a good Father that takes care of His children, we lose hope and turn to other things that this world tells us will fix the problem – that will heal the wound.

But the void in my life was never filled. The wounds of my past were never healed. Even though some of the feeling around the wounds went numb for a while, the pain was just covered up by things that would soon fade away. It was not gone. I was not healed. The destruction in my life generated by the past had not been repaired. And these things I was turning to were definitely not providing me the satisfaction I thought they would.

And soon, that truth would shine brighter than ever to me. That "aha moment" was just around the bend.

This Isn't Who I Am

———— ✣ ————

*I used to think a life free of inhibitions would lead to happiness;
but now I realize it only results in waking up feeling absolutely
empty.*

IT WAS JUST another night and just another party. My two close friends at the time and I got all done up – makeup, hair, outfit and all – and were heading out for the night. We were expecting a crazy party, since the guy who was hosting it had a famous reputation. Plus, it was one of the last nights of the summer. What better reason did we need to have a little more fun than usual? After one too many drinks, I arrived at a state that I rarely let myself get to: one where almost all of my inhibitions were gone.

My friend who was hosting this huge party had invited his (much) older brother who was in town, and we happened to start talking. I had seen him across the room earlier on; to say I was happy he came over to talk to me was an understatement. After a couple minutes, he led me upstairs to "give me a tour" of what I considered a mansion. (PS: to all my girls out there – don't trust a guy at a party who says he wants to give you a tour.)

We ended up walking into one of the guest bedrooms, as he began showing me all the different areas. It was huge. I couldn't believe this was just one of his family's guestrooms. *What does your room look like then?!* I thought to myself. At first, I didn't think twice about the situation I was currently in. I was completely fine; I could handle myself. Although I hardly knew what was going on. But I was also used to being alone with a guy. Like I said, I knew how to handle myself. Sadly, it wasn't anything new. But then things began escalading, and I found myself in a position I had promised myself I wouldn't get into.

That is when I heard a loud voice in my head, "Get up Sarah Grace. Get out of here. This isn't what you want. Don't make this mistake. GET UP AND LEAVE."

Without any of my own inhibitions still at play, something rose up within me, and—without being able to identify exactly what was happening in my current state—I immediately got up. I felt a strength I knew was not my own, and I got up right then and there before things went down the path I had promised myself I would never go down. The guy begged me to stay by using every cute line in the book. But I just kept saying, "No, no, I've got to go. I've got to find my friends. I have to go." I quickly got myself together, pushed the door wide open, and ran down the glass spiral staircase where I found one of my friends freaking out. She had been looking all over for me for the last hour.

That was the last of those nights. It was the last of the drinking, the guys, and the "fun life" behind my mother's back.

I woke up the next morning, and tears began flooding my eyes. *How had I fallen so far*, I wondered? I had almost given away the one part of myself I had always promised I never would, the one value that had stuck with me through all the years: my purity. And whatever my intentions were as I walked up those stairs that night, I can't blame anyone but myself. I had chosen to get to the state of mind I had been in that night.

But God was, and still is, great and faithful until the end. I know it was He that night who gave me strength to say no, to stand up, and to get out. Even when I was running from Him in the opposite direction, He faithfully stuck by my side and prevented something I would have regretted my whole life. I was living a life that basically spit in His face, saying, "I don't care." Yet, He never stopped loving me. He never gave up on me. As any good Father would do, He continued to pursue me and fight for me.

His love never fails. It's like the words in a popular song "Your Love Never Fails" by Jesus Culture:

> Nothing can separate
> Even if I ran away
> Your love never fails
> I know I still make mistakes
> But You have new mercies for me everyday
> Your love never fails

I may have been lying in bed still that morning, but my mind was running: *This isn't who I am, and it certainly isn't who I want to be. I don't even enjoy this life.* This whole new-Sarah-Grace lifestyle was one big game of pretending, of trying to fit in, and of running from my pain and the truth. I knew I needed to change. I wanted to go back to my roots, to the faith I had been raised in.

I finally wanted genuine change. I had been stuck in the denial phase for way too long. It's crazy how no one can help you until you truly *want* to be helped. From both my own experience and from talking to friends who watched me struggle through that time, I've come to realize It can be one of the most painful things to watch: a friend or family member go through something or hurting themselves in some way, knowing nothing you say will help until that person hits rock bottom and wants to change. I had finally reached that point; I had hit rock bottom. I desperately wanted to change. And God had prearranged an earthly source to help me do just that. *God, you are so good. You knew exactly what you were doing when you had me sit in the third seat of the last row in Math Studies this past spring.*

I quickly called Emily and told her I wanted to go to church with her. That I needed to talk – like really talk. More importantly, I told her that I wanted to be friends. Thinking back, that probably sounded weird to her. I'm sure she was thinking, *I thought we were friends?* After hanging up, I felt a joy and a freedom that I hadn't felt in a long time. That phone call was a monumental moment, as small as it may seem. It led to me recommitting to a personal, love relationship with my Savior and to me starting a lifelong friendship with another girl who loved Christ with all of her heart.

I had gone to church almost every single Sunday of my life, and truly had accepted Christ to be my Savior; but I had never really known what it meant to have a personal relationship with the Lord. I thought going to church and following the dos and don'ts was all it was about.

I was so wrong. The church I started attending with Emily opened my eyes to the truth that being a Christian wasn't about a religion or about some set of rules. It wasn't about how good you could be or about how many times you did or didn't mess up. No, it was about so much more. And, goodness, was I glad; because I had certainly messed up more than once. I wasn't perfect, and I knew I never would be—which is why this new perspective of Jesus was so freeing. It was about a personal relationship, one where I could communicate with and feel the presence of God. It was a love relationship with Jesus Christ...the same one that—no matter how far I had tried to run from—was always there to pick me up when I fell or cried out for help.

I was finally beginning to understand. God had opened my eyes and heart in a way I never would have imagined. And the greatest aspect of it all to me was that He didn't hold my past against me. After coming to Him with a sincere heart and desire for relationship, His grace enveloped me.

For I will forgive their wickedness and
will remember their sins no more. (Hebrews 8:12)

Life Is Real, not Perfect

I used to create a perfect picture in my mind of how everything would play out; but now I realize that is what messes us up most in life.

As I BEGAN my senior year, I was finally on the right track once again. I was feeling great.

Was it easy to change my life around completely? You might think it would be, since I had been so unhappy in the lifestyle I had been living. And at first, it was. The excitement of this new pursuit of Jesus distracted me from the pain I would soon face. Pain? Yes, pain. Changing meant giving up almost all of my friends. It meant abandoning all of my old ways of doing just about everything. It meant surrendering most of the things I did every weekend—and that was certainly not easy. Change is never easy, even when it's the healthy move for your life.

Usually a person's senior year of high school is the year when you feel the most loved, the most cared for, the most "popular"; you are the top dog now. You feel the closest to the friends you've made, since it is the fourth year you have been together now. But this wasn't the case for me. In the beginning of this season of change as senior year started, I felt alone. Instead of feeling closer than ever to all my friends that had been a part of my life the last four years, I was feeling distant. I was no longer hanging out with them on weekends. I was no longer contributing to the conversations they were having. And as much as I knew that distancing myself was the healthy decision, it was anything but easy. But I knew who

I wanted to be and the direction I wanted my life to go, and I knew participating in those things wouldn't lead me there. As I recently posted on Instagram, "difficult roads usually lead to beautiful destinations". Yet even in knowing the only relationship that truly mattered was with Christ and that He was always by my side – I was still lonely.

Even though I knew I was finally doing what was good for my life, I felt like I was lost. Everything was so new to me; and I felt that, besides my mom, I had no company on this new journey. Yes, I had been reaching out to and spending some time with Emily, but you can only feel so close to someone that you became friends with just a couple months ago. I wanted that *best-friend* relationship. I longed for that huge group of friends to do stuff with on the weekends again. But my schedule hardly allowed for such friendships to be created at this point. I was dedicating more time than ever to training for my last cross-country season; I was rarely on the same schedule as other high-school students. Waking up at 4:30 a.m. and being in bed by 10:00 p.m. didn't leave me much time or energy to strengthen new friendships. However, even though my loneliness caused some of the pain in my life, there was another source creating even more agony at the moment.

Running. That was the cause of my greatest emotional pain and heartache recently. No matter what I did, my races were ending awfully. And with each terrible race result, my confidence and self-esteem suffered as well. It was an inverse relationship. As my times increased, my confidence decreased. This in turn, only led to worse results the next race. It was a vicious cycle.

I had just completed an incredibly tough summer of training, waking up and running with my coach before our team would meet at 8:00 a.m.; then my coach would have me run the team workout as well. I had increased my mileage more than ever before, and had felt amazing coming into the season.

I thought I was finally doing everything right: training with all my heart, eating right and taking care of my body, and walking with Christ. The problem is that none of it seemed like it was paying off, and the stars weren't aligning like I thought they would. Train hard + love Jesus → achieve success. That is what I thought would happen. But even though I was completing the first part of that equation, the second wasn't happening. Things weren't just not ending as expected in races; they were going terribly.

However, I continued the morning routine I had started since changing my life: getting up thirty minutes early in order to dive into God's word before I started my day. Here is a glimpse from my journal that gives some insight to that time in my life:

Journal Entry: October 20ᵗʰ, 2010

I had early running practice this morning but then off-campus my first period,

so I came to Panera to read my Bible. God's been showing me so much this week. I've been really trying to surrender myself completely to Him, especially in my running. I just need to keep strong through these hard times of not doing well in races and keep having faith. I was starting to feel so defeated last week, and even didn't race the prestate meet because of not being able to sleep four nights in a row. I'm so embarrassed that I just told everyone I was sick. What's gotten into me? Mentally, I'm so defeated. I need to focus my mind on God and not on my performance. Jesus, help me to concentrate on the only thing that's important, You, and stop focusing on myself. Give me peace about this all, knowing that no matter how the rest of this season goes, You have a plan in it all.

That morning, I came across two verses that gave me renewed hope:

> But those who hope in the LORD
> will renew their strength.

They will soar on wings like eagles;
they will run and not grow weary,
they will walk and not be faint. (Isaiah 40:31)

So do not fear, for I am with you; do not be dismayed, for
I am your God. I will strengthen you and help you; I will
uphold you with my righteous right hand. (Isaiah 41:10)

I am not going to lie, I was thinking, *Wow, God is so great! He will be my strength, and I will give Him the glory as I reach my highest potential in running.*

But that didn't happen. For basically my entire cross-country season I continued to struggle. That season I had been running workouts that proved I could run times a minute faster than I was running in races. But for some reason, when I got on that starting line, something would happen to me mentally. I would slowly fade—feeling as if I had no energy—to the back of all the runners, running times slower than I had in practice. I didn't know what was wrong with me. I thought I was doing everything right. As I continued to have disappointing results, my mind-set changed, and I became filled with stress and anxiety before every race.

I began to look at the races as something *I* had to run on my own. Something that *I* was going to have to endure and be embarrassed about. Even though I would say in my mind that I depended on Christ for my strength and would give Him all the glory, *He* knew me better than I knew myself. He knew that I wasn't ready yet for what He had in store for me in my future. Every race continued to have the same results throughout the season. I would be ranked first, I would sprint out and be in first place for the first few minutes, and then I would mentally and physically give up, slowly being passed by one runner after the other. It was a very embarrassing time for me, and my pride was crushed. I felt the pity in the looks from friends and family post race. I had gone from feeling like the best runner in the state in the summer training sessions to feeling like I wasn't a threat to any of the top runners. Every race pushed me lower and lower mentally, and I slowly stopped believing in myself altogether.

Journal Entry: 10/10/10

So today's conference meet was yet another disappointment, even after feeling focused, praying to God beforehand, and feeling such a peace about the entire thing. I thought I was going to do great, and then it happened again; I gave up mentally and fell back. It's just so embarrassing. I was ranked number one at the beginning of the season, and now I'm not even ranked. No one believes in me anymore, just like I don't believe in myself. I just want this season to be over.

One good thing though: T was really encouraging to me after the meet and gave me a verse that really gave me hope. "Come to me, all you who are weary and burdened, and I will give you rest" (Matthew 11:28). I'm so thankful God has brought him into my life. He's been such a great friend, and we may even both sign with the University of Florida!

A Disappointment Gone Right

I used to think that God was all seriousness; but now I see that He has a sense of humor too.

YOU MAY BE wondering about that reference in my journal entry above... someone who I will refer to as "T." Don't worry, you'll find out all about T in a later chapter.

About this time in the season, I had been looking at colleges where I might run the coming year. Throughout high school I had said that I would never run in college; but my heart and mind-set changed as I began walking with Christ, and suddenly I felt a desire to run in college. Even though it was a late decision (most athletes begin talking to colleges their junior year), I reached out to some of the colleges that had sent me letters at the beginning of senior year.

I began getting so excited about all these far-away schools wanting me to come for a visit. *Wow UNC? Wait, I could probably go to an Ivy League?* But then my coach gave me some very wise advice that I will always be thankful for: "Choose to run for a school that you would want to attend even if you weren't running; you never know what will happen."

Being my first choice—whether I would be running or not—was the University of Florida. That was the school my mind had been set on long before running came into the picture. My big brother has been a huge gator fan since he was a boy, and I always wanted to do whatever he did. He even wrote the letters *U* and *F* on each of his cheeks when he was little, proud to be a gator fan. Unfortunately, he used a mirror to get the letters just right, and we all know how mirrors reflect backward. My mom was horrified when he came out with FU written on his cheeks! But, in all seriousness, UF had been my school of choice since I visited my brother there when he chose that college.

Earlier in the season our team had run at a meet that University of Florida hosted. I remember being so excited to prove my talent, as I knew the UF coach would be watching our race. The gun went off, and I sprinted to the front. This was a bold move for me with my recent race history. Unfortunately, as with every other year I had raced there, my performance on this course would once again turn into a horrible memory.

My freshman year was the first year I had run cross-country, and the race at the University of Florida was our first race of the season—my first race ever. I started the race full of excitement and ended…well, let me just say it is a good thing I even finished. From my initial state of excitement, I quickly did a one-hundred-eighty-degree turn into a state of doubt, frustration, and pain. I found myself thinking, *Why did I ever begin running? This is horrible. I want to quit. Can I stop and just say my knee hurts?*

My sophomore year I couldn't compete. That was when my weight had reached an all-time low, and I had been pulled from the team. When my junior year arrived, I was convinced that I would have a better experi-ence than I had my freshman year, and I was thankful I was able to run again and that I was at a healthy weight again. As usual, I sprinted when the gun went off. However, as we rounded the first extremely tight turn, a runner in our tight pack clipped my ankles from behind, and I went flying. I'm almost positive I did a complete somersault when I hit that grassy golf course. The rest of the race was a blur filled with hyperventilating, anger, and self-pity about the fact that I had been tripped. Needless to say, that race also ended in a very poor finish.

So, as you can see, when I sprinted to the front my senior year, I was certainly being bold. Unfortunately, the same thing happened as in every other race that season. I fell back as I second-guessed my ability, result-ing in yet another unfortunate finish. I crossed the line just happy the race and the embarrassment were over.

One thing I have learned about running is that it isn't like other sports where the worse you play, the less playing time you get. In run-ning, the worse you do, the longer "playing time" you get...and not in a good way.

Maybe still making the top thirty in each race wouldn't qualify as "terrible" to some; but for the perfectionist Sarah Grace who was ranked in the top five coming into this senior year season, it was hu-miliating. No one else put pressure on me to finish well, but I placed enough stress on myself to make up for everyone else. I was used to things coming easy to me. I was used to never failing. I hated feeling like I was disappointing someone. And by not finishing as I was ranked on paper to, I felt I was just that – a disappointment.

But despite coming in 22nd when ranked #1, I had a surprise visit upon finishing that race at the University of Florida that day. I was sit-ting near the finish line alone, gulping water, and inwardly analyzing why I had run so horribly again, when I heard a "hey!" It was none other than the University of Florida cross-country coach! Part of me couldn't be more excited, but as I quickly remembered how I had just run, embarrassment rushed over me. I struggled to catch my breath and to remain positive while the coach began asking me about the race, my college decisions, and about the possibility of me running for them.

I was dumbfounded. *What? Do you have the right girl? Did you just see how I ran? You must be blind. Are you crazy?* I had just run a terrible race, and my other races that season hadn't been very eye-catching either. So what attracted him to the nothing-special, struggling runner, Sarah Grace Spann? *God, you have such a sense of humor. You knew this would make me realize Your power and that this was all You, since it couldn't have been because I am a great runner and highly sought after by colleges*, I thought to myself.

It wasn't long afterward that I had some phone conversations and e-mail exchanges with the coach and found myself excitedly driving to Gainesville in late October for my official visit. This was a weekend visit where the coach gave me an opportunity to meet the team and trainers, hear about their training philosophy, see the facilities for the athletes, and see the campus on a more intimate basis.

That was a very special weekend, for more than one reason.

An Unexpected Message

I used to look for a guy to date everywhere I went; but now I realize that the saying is true: "You find someone when you're least expecting it."

MY WEEKEND AT University of Florida wasn't special because I fell in love with the program and school, like you may be thinking (even though I did). What made it truly special was someone I met during that weekend visit. Okay, I would be lying if I said that was the first I had ever heard of this young man. He was the "boy in blue from Charlotte High" that every girl on my team thought was cute. This boy had also happened to have sent me a message (or two) on Facebook a couple weeks before the official date of the weekend prospective students visited. After a few messages back and forth, I was happy to find out he would be going to the University of Florida the same weekend that I would be there. Here is a peek at our Facebook conversation:

Sarah Grace Spann   10/11, 9:04pm

most definitely,basically just gonna run from the finish line to my car haha. ahh thats no fun, but i guess going on a college visit makes up for it, where are ya going?

 ▆▆▆▆▆▆   10/11, 9:06pm

checking out UF 😃 are you looking anywhere around here?

 Sarah Grace Spann   10/11, 9:10pm

haha thats so weird, I have to call the UF coach tomorrow because he wants me to come up for a visit soon! but other then that im not sure..Ive been talking to the UCF coach but i dont really think I'd wanna go there out of all the schools

 Sarah Grace Spann   10/11, 10:40pm

haha oh I don't know,but hey,I might be coming up to UF that weekend too..because I think he told my coach either the 23rd or 30th

 ▆▆▆▆▆▆   10/11, 10:40pm

come the 23rd! that's when i'm going lol

 Sarah Grace Spann   10/11, 11:01pm

ahh I don't know if I can that weekend because I having my birthday party the 24th!

 ▆▆▆▆▆▆   10/11, 11:02pm

oh gotcha, well when you decide let me know 😃

 Sarah Grace Spann   10/11, 11:04pm
I willl 😃

 Sarah Grace Spann   10/12, 5:05pm

So I talked to the UF coach, and I'm gonna come up for my visit the 22nd and 23rd!sooo I guess we'll be up there at the same time

 ▆▆▆▆▆▆   🗔 10/12, 5:34pm

Yay:) I'm going up Thursday night, it stinks that we'll be missing the football game, I think we're actually playing you guys for homecoming night

 Sarah Grace Spann   10/12, 5:41pm

Oh really?but yeahh thats annoying,I can't believe you have to miss homecoming!but I'm glad Ill know at least one person up there 😃 do you think the guys and girls team will do things together or separately?

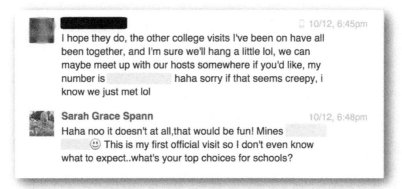

Oh, the classic Facebook messages! Those were actually the only ones I received from a random guy that I did *not* think were creepy.

As I said, we did end up attending the same weekend—in spite of my birthday party. And while that weekend in Gainesville may not have been the first time we talked, it was definitely when I saw something special in T.

I didn't realize at the time of the visit just how much I liked T, as I was so captivated by everything that weekend had to offer; but I did know I had met an awesome guy who I could potentially be teammates with the next year, and I knew we would get along great. We saw a lot of each other that weekend, as we were always with the coach, being shown all the University of Florida had to offer. And, in the process of our tours, we were able to get to know each other quite well. I remember even feeling comfortable enough to poke fun of T. We were sitting in the guidance counselor's office, and she began mentioning that there were options available for those who had special needs. I nudged his side and gave him a little "that's for you!" look. He just gave me a little smile and seemed a bit surprised that I felt comfortable enough to make a joke like that without really knowing him. Looking back, I can see that my behavior was immature and rather embarrassing.

But I knew there was something special about that boy that I liked a lot.

Remaining True

I used to love "playing the game" to get a guy's attention; but I soon realized I craved nothing more than to be transparent and authentic.

AFTER THAT WEEKEND, T and I continued to stay in touch by phone, and we began to encourage and inspire each other in our running. In the past, my conversations with guys had been superficial. But this time was different. I didn't feel like there were any games being played on either end.

Life is funny. All throughout high school, I had been looking for a guy to date, and I had never found one. And then my senior year came around, and I told myself that I wouldn't date because I figured I was about to leave for college and should focus solely on growing with Christ. Then, low and behold, He brought someone into my life unexpectedly.

As cliché as it may sound, it really was when I wasn't looking that Christ brought the perfect person for that time of my life into my path. T and I continued motivating each other, talking on the phone, and texting back and forth throughout the following weeks. I remember my friends saying in school, "You're texting him, aren't you?" They could always tell because I wore a huge smile on my face.

The feelings I was experiencing were very different for me. I had always been an independent girl who, as I said, "didn't need a guy to complete me." I was always the one my girlfriends would talk about, saying,

"Sarah Grace, why not him?" or "We need to find you someone." But I wasn't into dating just to date. I didn't need someone to make me happy. And call me selfish, but I surely wasn't going to invest the time in a guy who I couldn't possibly see myself with in the long run. That would only result in heartbreak, wasted time, and a lot of effort being put into something unhealthy.

As one of my favorite Christian YouTubers and writers, Jeff Bethke, said once in a Facebook status: "Dating without the intention of getting married is like going into the grocery store without money. You either leave unsatisfied, or you take something that isn't yours." I saw that dynamic happen around me all the time. I wasn't going to be another casualty of it.

But this friendship was different. Right from the beginning I promised myself that I would be completely open with T as to where I was in my walk with God. If he thought it was weird or decided to stop talking to me, well then, I knew it wasn't a relationship I wanted to be in anyway.

That decision made me nervous at first, because of course I wanted him to like me, but I knew deep down I wanted to stay true to myself for once. In the few relationships I had in the past, God had never been the center, and I wanted that to change. I had to trust that if this relationship was right, it would work out with me being fully transparent. It was uncomfortable to talk about my faith to someone I barely knew, as living a Christian lifestyle was still fresh to me. But I knew I never wanted to get involved with someone who didn't have the same values as I now had, so—trusting God that it would all work out—I went for it.

The result was amazing. T was almost in the same place in his life! He respected my beliefs and values more than I could have ever imagined. I remember one specific conversation on the phone—our first, more serious conversation. The topic of our past was brought up, and I became really nervous: nervous that T would judge me for my past or that he didn't hold the same values I did. As for the issue of sexual purity, if anyone could understand about messing up in the past, it would be me. But after committing to purity myself, it would definitely be a big plus to have someone who shared my beliefs…which is why the next question that came up in our conversation made me really nervous.

He asked what my belief about sexual purity was—not directly of course, that would be kind of weird and random. Remember, this was one of our first, longer phone conversations. I don't even remember how the subject came up, but in context, I promise you it wasn't out of nowhere. But all of a sudden, I felt myself get nervous about answering truthfully. *This is a choice I made myself, so why am I so nervous?* I thought. *Oh yeah, because—unlike in my grandma's time—in this society, I was definitely the minority for keeping such a promise.* What if T's beliefs were different? Would my stance be a deal breaker for him? I wanted him to like me. But after quickly analyzing the situation, I realized I wasn't about to get involved with someone who didn't know the *real* me. So I stayed true to myself and responded, "I am staying pure until marriage."

Then came the silence that made my heart just stop. In reality, it was probably only about a two-second pause, but to me it felt like a lifetime as I waited to hear how T would answer. That is when he spoke the response I never thought I would hear from a guy: "I am too."

My heart leaped for joy as I remembered God's faithfulness in saving me that one night at the party. I felt so thankful as, without Him showing up that night and giving me strength to walk away, I wouldn't have been able to say I was saving sex for marriage. One night's mistake would have led to years of regret.

As the weeks went by, T and I continued to say we were just friends, but we began getting to know each other more and more through our conversations. I had always felt like I had to pretend I was someone I was not with guys in the past, but not with T. I could be completely myself, and the best part was that he not only supported and valued everything I stood for, but he made me want to become a better person.

I felt myself growing not only closer to T but closer to God. T and I encouraged each other not only in our running but in our walks with Christ too. Earlier in the year, I had felt so alone as I began this new spiritual journey of mine, but not anymore. Through sending Bible verses back and forth and having long talks about what we had learned in our reading that morning, I couldn't help laughing with joy as I looked up to God with thankfulness.

You are surely a good God who will always provide me everything I need. This is the start of something new...something that is really incredible, I thought to myself.

Journal Entry: 11/01/10
Jeremiah 29:11: "For I know the plans I have for you," declares the LORD, "plans to prosper you and not to harm you, plans to give you hope and a future."

This verse just really spoke to me and gave me such encouragement. I find myself having doubts and fears in my running abilities and future, but I realize I need to have faith that God has it all under control and has a great plan for me. If I truly trusted Him, I wouldn't have any fears. I wouldn't fear not being number one in running or where I will pick to go to college or what will come of my relationship with T...I need to have complete faith, make Him my focus, and stop caring about how all the little things will work out. Even though I'm going through a tough time in my running, I need to keep "eagerly awaiting," like Galatians 5:5 says, and know that God will be my provider and strength.

On a side note: I think God really has placed T in my life for a reason. It's crazy how I've always looked for someone or would get super sad when things didn't work out with someone else...but now that I wasn't looking, he just comes into my life unexpectedly (through a FB message! Ha ha). He's everything I could want in a guy and the first guy I have been completely open with and shared my faith with...which makes me like him that much more. It seems like he truly loves God and always says the sweetest things to me. I just hate the hour drive between us. But it's so crazy we may end up being at UF together if we both sign there! Guess everything happens for a reason. ☺

Humble Confidence

I used to fear being confident; but now I see that was an issue of pride.

THE WEEKS FLEW. Soon enough, it was down to crunch time in my running realm. States was just around the bend, and districts and regionals were now approaching. But unlike other years—or even earlier in that season—I felt like I was finally getting back to a healthy place, both mentally and spiritually.

Earlier in the fall, I could barely sleep before races because of the pressure I put on myself to accomplish my big goals. But now I was giving it all to Jesus, resting securely in the fact that—no matter what—He had a plan to prosper me. I knew that whatever happened, everything would be okay. Most importantly, I now had realized that running *was not* everything in life. It may seem silly, but subconsciously, I had felt that if I didn't succeed in running—whether in a workout or in a race—I was a failure. Thankfully, that was no longer my mentality.

With the encouragement I was getting through my daily quiet times spent in God's word, and the words I was receiving from T, I was beginning to feel like myself again, in all areas. I had what I would like to call an extra pep in my step. I had a new excitement about life in general—instead of being stressed about running, anxious about college decisions, and unhappy about past races. As I truly began laying down all my worries and anxiety at the foot of the cross of Jesus, I felt as if a burden had been lifted.

And in case you are wondering, no, my new "pep" did not come from races going better for me. There was no instant change in my race results, but I could feel that I was different, and I knew my time was coming. For once—deep in my heart—I began to believe in myself and in the power of my God.

> *Journal Entry: 11/04/10*
>
> *My faith has grown so much lately. I think I'm finally starting to put my complete faith in God. I see my mind-set changing so much for the good. I used to never want to say I think I will win or that I know I'll do good, because I had such a lack of faith in God and such low self-esteem. I was constantly filled with doubt. But now I know that when I have Christ in me, all things are possible. I need to continue to speak words of faith, even when things aren't going well still. I need to act like I've already received what I've asked for.*
>
> *Philippians 1:20: "I eagerly expect and hope that I will in no way be ashamed, but will have sufficient courage so that now as always Christ will be exalted in my body."*

The next morning after I wrote that journal entry, I opened my Bible as usual to begin my quiet time. Have you ever come to a verse just at the right time? One that may not have had any significance on any other given week or day but had great meaning to you right in that moment? That was the case the morning I opened to this verse:

> For if you remain silent at this time, relief and deliverance for the Jews will arise from another place, but you and your father's family will perish. And who knows but that you have come to your royal position for such a time as this? (Esther 4:14)

To give a little context for those who don't know the story, this verse is about Esther, a Jewish woman. Back in that day, a Jewish woman would have never been selected to be a queen. Yet. even though she was a Jew, she had found favor in the king's eyes and was made queen as a result. These words were saying that Esther was given her royal position for a reason and that she should use it for Christ and to save her Jewish people.

But Esther's actions came with risks—literally being killed (for that was the consequence of approaching the king without being asked, even if you were the queen). And even though I definitely had no reason to fear being killed (aren't you thankful for the people who have fought to give us that freedom here in America?), I immediately felt that Christ was telling me to use my position for His good.

I felt Him saying that I held the position as team captain and had been given talent that the other girls looked up to for a reason. I was given this talent so that I could use it for the Lord, not so that I could lift myself up or have people think I was anything great. I began feeling a sense of conviction, a feeling that I had not fully used the position I was given to its fullest potential so far. I felt God telling me that before the next race, when our team huddled together, I should ask to pray with everyone.

You may be thinking, *Praying with your teammates wouldn't be so hard.* Some people can pray aloud without a second thought, but that was not the case for me. It scared me out of my mind to think about doing this. Yes, I loved the Lord, and I loved praying...but in front of people? I could hardly think of doing so. Doubts began creeping into my mind, fear that my teammates would all think I was weird. Or worse, I feared they would think I was hypocritical. They had known the old partying me and how I used to live. I was scared, and I didn't know if I could do it.

Journal Entry: 11/05/10

Esther 4:14... just wow. I feel like lately God has been calling me to be a light to my team. I'm not just captain for no reason. Last year, I didn't think anything of it. But now I realize my days are short, and I need to use every single day to "store up treasures in heaven" and not just work for things here on earth. I feel like God wants me to pray with my team as we huddle together before the district race, but that makes me so nervous. Hopefully, if I can do it, opportunities will come of it! God's been showing me His power so much. I've been praying to have a craving for reading His word and only for Him and no one else, because last year that certainly wasn't the case. But I truly do crave to read the Bible each morning I wake up now. It's crazy. He answered my prayer for sure. And with making so many important decisions about colleges and everything soon, I need to be in constant communication with Him more than ever so that I can follow His will. I don't want to pick a college just because of a person or because it "makes sense." We will see! Anyway, I'm tired, but the district race is this weekend! Let's go!

I Will Follow

I used to think winning would equal happiness; but now I realize that following God's voice offers much more joy than any medal could.

IT WAS TIME to face the district meet.

This was the first race that counted toward reaching our ultimate goal as a team—and as individuals: the state race. I typically would get wrapped up in anxiety and nervous knots the night before a race. Even melatonin didn't help me sleep. (Yes, I had tried any and every OTC sleep aid with the constant struggle I was having that year). Insomnia was the worst feeling. I would lie in bed at night, knowing I needed to fall asleep so that I could wake up early and feel rested and ready to race my best...Yet, I would lay in my bed wide awake for hours. And when this pattern continued each week, it became worse because then I was mentally psyching myself out about falling asleep. Been there? If you have, you know what I mean. It is a true struggle. Many nights, I would find myself wanting to scream with frustration, wondering why I couldn't fall asleep when I felt so physically exhausted. But my mind would continue to run. There was no off button.

However, morning of the district race came, and unlike every other night before a race, I was able to sleep well. So that morning already felt different from the moment I woke up; I got out of bed rested and ready. I read my Bible as I drank my hot tea and ate my peanut butter toast, and began getting ready to leave for the race. Of course, I had to spend extra time getting ready so that I looked good no matter how early it was since T would be there with his team too. (And that time spent was well worth it; we got our first photo together taken that day.)

When I was feeling ready and had everything packed, my mom and I got in her car, and off we drove into the sunrise towards the District course. The starting time of the race got closer, and it was almost time to get ready to line up on the starting line when my team huddled together to shout our typical pump-up cheer. I think it went something along these lines: "*S-U-P-E-R*, super, super, that's what we are! *G-R-E-A-T*, super great we'll always be…*F-O-R-T*, Forrrrrt Myers!" We would start out chanting quietly and would then repeat the cheer louder and louder.

We made a scene every race, and the other teams would stop and stare at us. I secretly loved it.

But then I knew it was my time. I knew that I needed to do what I had felt Christ telling me I should do. Silently praying for God's strength, I nervously and abruptly blurted out, "Can I pray really quickly?" To my surprise, my teammates were all happy for me to proceed. I can't even recall exactly what that prayer was, but I'm sure it wasn't one of my most eloquent moments. I was as nervous as I could be. I'm sure some of you can relate. You take the time to plan exactly what you want to say to someone and have it all rehearsed, but as soon as you open your mouth, you get nervous, and it all goes down the drain. But I knew I was following Christ's lead, and because of that, I felt excited after praying. No matter how awkward I may have sounded, I was ready to run that race now.

We lined up, the gun went off, I sprinted to the front. This is how every race this season had gone, except for in the past, I had dropped off, finishing way behind the front pack. I began repeating positive words to myself about how I wouldn't drop back this time. I sprinted ahead of the front pack and never looked back. After eighteen minutes and some seconds, I crossed that finish line—in first.

My heart could not have been happier. I felt like a little girl in a candy store. Okay, that isn't the best analogy. I've never been the best with comparisons. But I was ecstatic. I wasn't feeling elated solely because I won but because I had truly run to my potential and finally felt good while doing so. For the first time that season, I didn't have thoughts of quitting, or questions about why I ever began running in the first place, going through my mind.

For a girl who had struggled all season, a girl who had run slower times in races than she had in practices, a girl who had thoughts of quitting before crossing the finish line every race prior (a.k.a., me)...finishing the race with a good time was huge. And I knew God had been with me that race. Well, He had been with me every race, but I was finally believing He was there now, and I was running in faith.

I couldn't wait to continue to the next level as a team: regionals.

Journal Entry: 11/09/10
This weekend at districts, I finally asked my team to pray before we got on the line! I was so nervous and probably sounded quite awkward...but I felt so good after doing it. God definitely helped me and gave me courage. And guess what? I won! With God's strength and not my own, I did it finally! (Because we all know Sarah Grace over here hasn't had any strength this whole season.) Through this tough season, God has really shown me how weak and powerless I am on my own without Him. I just have this good feeling inside of my heart. Like that I have struggled as much as I have this season so that He can bring me to the top, and everyone will know it was a miracle. But I may be

getting too ahead of myself. Anyway, I have regionals this coming weekend, and it'll be super tough competition. This course is already hard, and now they added a sand pit to the mix. Gee, how thoughtful to us runners. Ugh. I'm going to need Your strength once again, Jesus!

The Power of the Tongue

*I didn't used to believe in the power of the tongue and the words
you speak with it; but now I see that what you say has incredible
power and can change everything.*

THE RACECOURSE FOR the regional race was known to be extremely tough
and slow. And this year, as I mentioned in my journal, they decided to add
a huge sand volleyball court at the very end of the course that we had to
circle (staying *in* the sand). This was the last thing any of our legs wanted
at the end of the grueling racecourse.

I began to feel that familiar fear creep back. After finally having a
good race, I didn't want to go back to that feeling of failure that I had finished most races this season with. What if I fell back and ran slowly again?
What if I couldn't sleep the night before and felt exhausted the morning
of the race? All of these doubts began nagging me.

Every year I had run horribly on this course, and with the addition of
the sand, I definitely wasn't looking forward to it. I began talking negatively about how hard the sand was going to be and how I didn't know
how the race was going to go for me. In mid sentence my mom stopped
me, saying, "Sarah Grace, words are very powerful. Speak what you want
to happen, and believe that God will have it come to pass. Never speak
negatively." In the way most teens react to their parent's life lessons, I
nodded my head in agreement, but I questioned the accuracy of her
theory of the power of words.

Clearly, I didn't believe she was too accurate because I continued to say negative things. I'd like to think that I did believe in my ability to do well, somewhat. But I had such a bad habit of saying negative things when it came to myself and my own abilities that negative words just came out without thinking. If I'm honest, I will admit that I always felt it was better to expect the worst outcome, so that if situations (or my own performance) came out better, awesome! But if they didn't, I would be disappointed (and I wouldn't disappoint anyone else). Looking back, I see that was a self-confidence issue.

But that next week Momma Spann did everything in her power to change my thinking. Every time she heard me say something negative, or even when she thought I was thinking doubtful thoughts, she made me repeat this sentence loudly tens times (scream would actually be more descriptive): "The sand is my strength!" You can imagine my reluctance. "That's so embarrassing, Mom. No way, I'm not saying that. Okay, okay, I said it in my head," I would say to her. But she was persistent, and she finally got me to say "the sand is my strength" every time I thought or said something negative—no matter how silly I felt doing so.

And, yes, the negative self-talk stopped rather quickly after I started saying those words. Mom was always good about stopping my negativity using tactics like this, with any aspect of life.

The day of the regional race came. I woke up—thankful that I felt rested after a good night's sleep—and did my normal morning routine. I made my tea, sat down with my mug, and began reading my Bible; then I suited up in my green-and-white uniform, packed my bag, and left for the race. I felt the nerves coming and couldn't seem to get rid of them no matter how many positive things I said. There was tougher competition this time, but I couldn't let that shake my confidence.

That was the amazing thing about finding my confidence in Christ instead of myself, I realized. If I was counting on myself to show up and run that race on my own, there is no way I could have believed in a good end result. I had been counted out this season by not only myself but almost every other person who watched our races: other teams, parents of other teams, announcers, interviewers…You get the idea. After the results of the first half of my season, I would never be seen as a favorite to win a race this season. But after reading verses like "when I am weak, then He is strong" and how God's "power is made perfect in weakness" (2 Corinthians 12:9–10), I knew I could have confidence going into that race.

When I arrived at the course, I prayed with my teammates once again. The race started, and off we sprinted to take on that extremely tough course. Minutes passed slowly, and the hills were grueling. I fought as hard as I could to stay with the front pack, tempted to give in around the two-mile point. I felt like I was walking up those hills instead of running the second loop around the course. But I had stayed with the pack up until this point, and I wasn't about to surrender now. Then my legs began feeling heavy. The competition this time around was much greater than the previous weekend. Again, the pain almost convinced me to give in. And the sand…well, let's just say it felt more like quicksand than volleyball-court sand. But all front pack runners managed to cross the sand for the last time, and we rounded the last corner. The finish line was now in sight. I heard the footsteps of the other runner behind me, and saw two of the girls out of my peripherals beside me. It came down to the last .1 of this 3.1-mile race.

The "sand had been my strength," as I crossed the finish line in first, by the strength of God again.

Journal Entry: 11/12/10

I can't believe it. Here I sit laughing at my mom when she tells me to stop talking negatively and tries to make me say positive things out loud, but now I see the difference it makes! I won regionals! I am finally believing and having confidence—not in me, but in my God. I couldn't feel more positive. And it's not only because I won but because Jesus has changed my perspective completely, and winning is only the icing on top of an already happy life.

With Prayer and Petition

I used to try to fit in with the world around me; but now I realize
I'm called to stand out like an alien and do crazy things.

MY WINS BEGAN getting people's attention. The girl who had died in every race this season and was a mental case had now run two pretty strong races. But I still wasn't actually considered a threat for the state race.

T had also run a fantastic race at regionals that day, placing in the top three which wasn't new for him. He was the top runner on his team—and, typically, in the area—since his freshman year. After the race, T told me that he had decided to sign with the University of Florida and commit to running for them the next year. I was very excited for him (and for selfish reasons too, as he had received offers from many amazing schools around the nation, but this was the only school that we both might sign with). Even though I was tempted to make my own decision for UF right then and there, I knew I needed to continue praying. As close as T and I had grown over the past month and a half, I still needed to make the decision Christ was leading *me* to make. Plus, even though I was leaning toward UF, it would be silly to make such and important decision based on my short friendship with T.

My joy after finishing the regional race was quickly tempered by a scary thought: the state race was only a week away.

And being typical Sarah Grace, I began to let my nerves creep in once again. I mean, who wouldn't be nervous? I kept thinking about how highly

I was ranked my junior year and yet how terribly the race had ended. If I could be ranked in the top five and finish miserably, what would happen this year when I wasn't ranked at all?

The state course was never a favorite course of mine, and even though many runners had run their best times there, I couldn't say the same. As I described earlier, this race was run around a huge horse track. We made two loops around the huge, oval-shaped course, and the last quarter mile of the course was a slowly increasing, backbreaking, leg-shaking hill. (And of course they placed the finish line at the top.)

The week before the big race, a reporter who wrote for the biggest high-school running site on the Internet decided to interview me. I wish I could say that what he said to me surprised me, but after how my season had been going, it didn't. I remember our conversation very distinctly:

Interviewer: When I mentioned your name as a possible con-
tender for the state meet, my colleague stated that you are
only ranked twenty-ninth in the top times out of the state. But I
told him that I think you may be a dark horse in the night. What
is your response?
Me: Yes [laugh inserted], I know my ranking very well and where
I am expected to be in this weekend's race. But I also believe
anything is possible with Christ, and whatever His will is what will
happen Saturday.

Here are some quotes from the article that was written after our interview:

*"Well, it's been interesting and busy are probably the best words.
I had some of the best summer training I've ever been able to do,
put in a lot of mileage for the first time, and was really excited*

for **the** season. As the season came around, I had a couple of off races to begin with, which kind of messed me up mentally. As districts and regionals came up, I think I finally got back into it mentally, and with the help of God's strength, I feel like I've been doing better and better each week and am definitely ready for states."

So far this year, the Fort Myers senior has a season best of 18:37, only the twenty-ninth fastest time in the state. She reminds us not to be fooled by the numbers and knows the competition Saturday will be fierce.

"I'm fully aware my times haven't been the fastest this season, but I know I'm capable of so much more. It's just putting it all together for once and racing my race; we'll see what happens."

(Mile Split. (n.d.). Spanning The Student-Athlete Spectrum. Retrieved November 17, 2010, from http://fl.milesplit.com/ articles/55672-)

The reporter seemed stunned by my response and wasn't too sure how to take the whole God reference, I think. But he thanked me and wished me good luck. Of course, even though I was trying to maintain a positive mind-set and a confident demeanor in the interview, knowing that I was ranked twenty-ninth put a seed of doubt in my mind. I knew I hadn't run excellently that season, but to go from my junior year's ranking of top five to twenty-ninth was pretty humbling.

Thankfully, my mom was there as my rescue from negativity again. She reminded me of the verse that she had showed me way back during my sophomore year: "Then the LORD replied: *'Write down the revelation and make it plain on tablets so that a herald may run with it'*" (Habakkuk 2:2).

She also reminded me of Philippians 4:6: "Do not be anxious about anything, but in every situation, by prayer and *petition*, with thanksgiving, present your requests to God."

Petition was a key word in the verse that I had always overlooked. The Unabridged Merriam Webster Dictionary definition is this: "A formal written request, typically one signed by many people, appealing to authority with respect to a particular cause." My mom was always good about taking God's word and bringing it to life, making it applicable to us. And even though some may have seen her as overzealous at times (including myself), I couldn't be more thankful for what, at the time, I thought of as her craziness. She encouraged me to write my own, legitimate petition to Christ—not just to say a prayer, but to write a full document, print it, and sign it like a real petition.

If someone had told me to do this a year before, I would have laughed. But for some reason, when my mom encouraged me to write a petition to God, I was completely open to the idea. I was finally living in the faith of God and His power now, instead of my own. And I realized that when I was truly living for Him, I might do things that looked ridiculous to the outside world.

I began to search my Bible and write down all the verses I wanted to use in my petition. God offers us so many incredible promises in his word, but as my mom told me over and over again, we have to decree them over our lives. I realized I needed to do exactly that.

I typed my formal document to Christ, praying that He would give me the state champion title, as I wrote down all the promises He had given me as His child. I even created a place to sign and date it like an official document. Then, I printed it, signed my name, and dated it in ink. I reread that petition over and over each day before the state meet until, slowly but surely, I started believing with all my heart that God would help me to do what I was requesting.

Petition for State XC Race

Dear, Holy Father, the Father of my Lord Jesus Christ, your Word says in Philippians 4:6, *"Do not be anxious about anything, but in everything, by prayer and petition, with thanksgiving, present your requests to God.* So, I write this petition asking that **You will help me to win my 3A State race on Saturday, November 19, 2010 at the Little Everglades Ranch in Dade City @ 09:40.** I ask that *"the peace of God, which transcends all understanding, will guard my heart and my mind in Christ Jesus."* (Philippians 4:7) I ask that this peace would so envelope me and consume me that I would sleep like a baby the night before and wake up refreshed the morning of the race. I ask that *"You would be my confidence"* (Proverbs 3:26) in the race. I ask that *"I would not fear this vast army"* of competitors *"before me for it is You, O Lord, who arms me with strength.* (Deuteronomy 3:22) *"You make my feet like the feet of a deer."* (Psalm 18:32-33) I have done my part in physically training my body & leading a disciplined life. But, I need your supernatural anointing; and, I ask that you would *"anoint my head with oil"* for this occasion on Saturday, November 19th. (Psalm 23:6) And, I ask that You would **"give me your shield of victory"**. (Psalm 18:37) I ask that *"You will enable me to pursue my adversaries & overtake them"* if anyone gets in front of me (Psalm 18:37). I thank you that *"You show your loving kindness to your anointed."* (Psalm 18:50) In my own strength, winning this race seems impossible; but, I thank you *"that all things are possible to me because I believe in Jesus Christ"* and have the Holy Spirit living within me. (Matthew 19:26) I believe that Jesus Christ is your son, that he died for my sins, he rose from the dead and sits at your right hand *"far above all ruler, authority, power, dominion, name that has been given or will ever be given"*. (Ephesians 1:21) Because Jesus Christ lives, I know *"I can do all things through Christ who strengthens me"* (Philippians 4: 16). I ask that You would strengthen my body that day with the mighty force, that electrifying power You used when You raised Christ from the dead. I thank you that this same power is *"in me who believes"*. (Ephesians 1:19).

I pray *"no one will that be able to stand up against me"* on Saturday, November 19, 2010. (Joshua 1:5) I ask that by your anointing power, that *"I would trample them all"*. (Deuteronomy 34:29) I thank you that *"Your incomparable great power"* will consume me and shine through me this day. (Ephesians 1:18) I thank you that this power is greater than any physical power of man. I ask that You would make me *"the head"* (Deuteronomy 28:13)

When I come upon the place in the race that I feel like settling, I ask that *"Your strength would be made perfect in my weakness"*; that You would remind me to draw *"from Your incomparable great power that is in me"* (Ephesians 1:18) and that *"the power of Christ's glory would rest upon me"* (2Corinthians 9-10). I also ask that *"You will give strength to my weary body and increase my power... and renew my strength"* (Isaiah 40:28).

I declare that *"no weapon forged against me will prosper"* (Isaiah 54:17) for *"greater is He that is in me than he that is in the world"* (John 4:4). I claim by faith that *"Your Glory will be my rear guard "* (Isaiah 58:8) I bind every ruler, authority, power of darkness & spiritual force of evil that might try to come against me that day for "Matthew 16:19) says *"You have given me the keys to the kingdom of heaven and whatever I bind on earth You will bind in heaven"*. I renounce *"the spirit of fear"* for *"You did not give me a spirit of fear but of Power, love, truth & a sound- mind."* (2 Timothy 1:7) I ask that *"angels of the Lord would surround me"*. (Psalm 34:7) And, *"Father, I ask that You use all your heavenly resources to protect me from evil"* (Luke 22:31). I *"take every thought captive to the obedience of Christ"*. (2 Corinthians 10:3) Help me to speak no unbelief with my mouth or entertain thoughts of doubt. I believe that the *"Word of God that I speak will accomplish what I desire"* (Isaiah 55:11) for *"it is active and living and sharper than any double-edged sword"* (2Corinthians 10:3)

So, I ask that ***"You would make me stronger than my adversaries "*** (Psalm 105:24) and that You , O Lord, ***"will cause me to ride on the heights of the land"*** on Saturday, November 19, 2010. (Isaiah 58:14).

The writing of this petition is based upon the Word of our Lord which says:

Matthew 21:22   "If you believe, you will receive whatever you ask for in prayer."
John 15:16 "You chose me & appointed me that I should go and bear fruit and that my fruit should remain, that whatever I ask of the Father in Your name, You will give to me."

Matthew 18:19 "Again, I tell you that if two of you on earth agree about anything you ask for, it will be done for you by my Father in heaven. For where two or three come together in my name, there am I with them."

John 16:24b "Ask and you will receive and your joy will be complete."

This petition is made and signed this 17th day of November 2010 between Sarah G. Spann and Judith E. Spann, believers in our Lord and Savior Jesus Christ.

_____   _____
Sarah G. Spann   Judith E. Spann

Believing the Incredible

*I used to see quotes everywhere that running is 90 percent mental;
but now I think that could apply to life in general. It's all about
the mind.*

THE STATE MEET was about a three-hour drive from our city, so my team always drove up the day before. We would run the course as a shakeout run the day we arrived, and that is when all the nervous feelings and anxious thoughts began to penetrate my mind. I remember it like it was just yesterday. I was jogging around the horse track next to my teammates and coach. Even though I was having a funny conversation with them, I mentally began playing out every situation that could happen the next morning on that very course. But every time I caught myself thinking about a negative outcome, I quickly stopped myself and began creating a more positive vision.

We turned the corner of the horse track to enter the infield portion of the course. The infield of the horse track was always my weak point. It was at about the one-and-one-half to two-mile point of the race, and I always seemed to give up and fall back from the lead pack—especially the year before. I felt my heart sink like it had exactly one year ago when I fell back from the lead pack and realized that I was not going to finish the way I wanted to in that state race. I quickly began praying silently, asking God to allow this portion of the course to be my strength this year, despite what had happened every other time I had raced this course. I asked Him not only to be with me through this portion of the race but to *be* my portion, as Psalms 73:26 says He is and always will be.

What would help me get past that hard spot in the race where I always struggled and fell behind the pack? What would make me finally believe in myself...and in the power of my God?

My mind.

I had to believe in myself and in God's power. This was something I hadn't done other years (or even earlier that season), and it certainly did not come naturally to me. Running quotes always seem to say running is 90 percent mental, and after this not-so-encouraging season of mine, I couldn't have agreed more!

I think the power of the mind actually applies to way more than just running. Ninety percent of *life* is mental, when you really think about it. I've realized that if you're going to achieve anything in life, you have to do two things: you must believe, and you must persevere. An app of mine just reminded me of a Facebook status I posted the very night before the state race: "Faith sees the invisible, believes the incredible, and receives the impossible. States tomorrow, let's go, girls!"

After finishing our shake-out jog that day before the state race, we headed back to our hotel to get ready for dinner. We always had dinner the night before state at this specific restaurant. It was a cute, little, family-owned Italian restaurant called Papa Joe's. The food was great—although I had never had anything but the spaghetti and meatballs. That was a good, prerace carb meal.

Back at the hotel, as I was changing clothes and sprucing up to go to the restaurant, along with two of my teammates, they were joking around with me. "So, have you kissed T yet?" I laughed as I said no and tried to explain that we were just close friends for now (even though I clearly felt more strongly than that). We were simply two people seeing where time might lead. But the jokes kept coming. That was one thing my team was certainly good at the past couple weeks: embarrassing me in front of T and his team by making little remarks about the two of us. At any race where both he and my team were, my coach or teammates made sure to made a comment loud enough for the two of us to hear. (I secretly didn't mind it. But I acted like I wanted them to stop.)

We finished getting ready for dinner and hopped into the team van, and off to Papa Joe's we went. It would be the last visit for me after joining the tradition for the past three years. But I was extra excited this time around because T and his parents happened to be going there too. This wasn't really a big surprise, since Papa Joe's really was the only place for a good pasta meal in that little town. Through texts, T had told me he would be there. So I spent a little more time getting ready than I normally would have for a cross-country dinner. I was excited to see him, but I tried to hide it. Earlier in the week, I had written him a good-luck letter, including a Bible verse for his race and just letting him know how special our friendship was to me and how thankful I was for all of his encouragement and support. He was expected to be in the top finishers, and I wanted to give him all the encouragement I could to help him believe he could win.

I took the letter to dinner, but I hadn't told tell I had written something for him. I remember nervously sitting in the front of the restaurant as we were waiting for our huge party to be seated, wondering how I would go about giving him the letter, what I say when he first walked in, and how to talk to him without making a fool of myself.

T and his parents did arrive as expected, along with one of their good family friends who served as a coach and mentor in T's life. I nervously walked over and said hi to him, with all my teammates watching and making little jokes and remarks about how cute we were. I felt so embar-rassed. Then I sat down with my team at the table where we had been seated by that time, and I tried to have fun with my friends. I laugh as I remember how I purposefully tried to have fun in a loud way, in order to attract T's attention to our table. (Don't pretend like you haven't done that before.)

Later in the dinner, I texted T. No, I didn't have the guts to just go up to his table and talk to him as a normal human being would have. But I did want to make sure he would tell me when he was leaving, so I could come say bye before he left. (I knew his party of four would definitely be done before our party of about forty.) As our table was just getting our food, I got a text saying T was about to leave, and I anxiously got up and pulled the letter out of my pocket. He and his parents were standing outside the restaurant when I walked out. I think his parents realized I was coming to say good-bye, and they said, "We'll go get the car!" We both just smiled. I tried to avoid being awkward as much as I could, but I'm not sure I was very successful. We made small talk for a little while, and then we wished each other good luck for the big race the next morning. Our conversation was quite short, but it felt like forever. We weren't at the stage of having relaxed, unplanned conversations yet. Many times I had tried to plan what I was going to say, whether it be in person or on the phone. I'll admit it; I had back-up topics to talk about on the phone in case a long silence occurred.

Well this night wasn't different. I had tried to figure out exactly what to say when giving T the note and saying good-bye. Too bad that, as soon as I looked into his eyes, all those preplanned words disappeared from my mind. We began saying our good-byes, leaned in, (insert an awkward pause here), and then hugged. I pulled the note out of my pocket and handed it to him. He looked into my eyes and smiled. We said our sec-ond good-byes of the night. (Have you been there? The first good-bye didn't go quite right, so after the first awkward hug, a second good-bye is initiated?) But this time, as we leaned in, our lips met in a kiss instead of our arms in a hug.

I walked back into the restaurant happier than I had been in a very long time. When we were settled back in the hotel room after dinner, I was talking to the same girls who had been joking with me as we got ready for dinner. I smiled at them as I said, "You know that question you asked me earlier, before dinner? Well things have changed since my first answer..." And the biggest smile ever spread across my face.

Okay, it's time to get into my race mind-set Sarah Grace, I told myself. The rest of the night, any time a negative thought came into my mind, I'd combat it with five positive thoughts—a lesson from Momma Spann that was well learned by now.

Running by Faith and not by Sight

—— ⚬⚬ ——

I used to believe "all things were possible" except for some things,
putting limitations on the promise. But now I realize that when
Jesus said "all," He meant all.

THE BIG DAY had come.

My alarm rang early that morning, and I woke up immediately. I had slept in my mom's hotel room that night versus a room with my teammates in order to prepare mentally as best as possible, and I couldn't have woken up more refreshed. We sat side by side that morning and prayed, and then I read my Bible for a bit before getting ready. I decided I would pick a verse to write on my hand—something that could encourage me during the race when I thought of giving up. I wanted to remind myself why I was running this race in the first place when the pain in my legs set in.

I immediately knew the verse I was going to choose. Like I mentioned earlier, T and I had frequently sent inspirational verses back and forth in the weeks leading up to the race. One that he sent to me stood out. I pulled the permanent marker out of my bag and wrote down the verse.

All my hard work had come down to this day. But, ultimately, I knew it wasn't my hard work that would get me anywhere. No, it would be the Lord's work and strength. I read over my petition one last time before leaving my hotel room, full of faith. As I was walking out of the hotel toward my car, my teammate's sister found me and said, "T was staying at our hotel and made sure to find me so that I could pass on this note to you!" She handed me a handwritten note, all folded up. A big smile appeared on my face. Wow, he was the sweetest.

After reading T's encouraging note, full of caring and thoughtful words, a warmth came over me. Our initial notes to each other were pages long, and they definitely set the tone for the future because no note after those were any shorter! I appreciated those long notes so much. There is something special about handwritten, thoughtful letters—even more precious than a gift. I folded the note back and continued toward my car. I looked at my hand, and the verse written on it, as I was getting into my car and spoke the verse from memory: "Jesus looked at them and said, 'With man this is impossible, but not with God; all things are possible with God" (Mark 10:27).

I knew I could not win this race in my own strength. The fact that I was ranked twenty-ninth clearly showed that there were many runners with better times who were competing with me that day. But I had secret weapons that I wasn't sure they had. I had Christ on my side and a heart filled with faith. And with those, all things are possible.

The Final Minutes

—⟨ ⟩—

I used to think I would find unshakable confidence in my own capabilities; but now I realize it's only found in our unshakable God.

OUR TEAM CARAVAN pulled up to the racecourse as the sun was beginning to rise. It was always a beautiful experience. The orange and yellow colors rose over the horizon and onto the gigantic, green horse track. The silhouettes of the fence that lined the inside of the track, the smell of the freshly cut grass, the morning dew, and the empty, bare stands that would soon be holding a swarm of fans, family, and friends would all change in a few minutes. It is one of those moments that you wish you could just blink your eyes to take a photograph. Within what seemed like only a few moments, the sun was high in the sky, the heat pounding down, and crowds of people began to line up along the course.

This was a race where competitors left one of two ways: feeling down and disappointed or ecstatic and proud. In the past I had seen some runners walk by with loud voices and happy expressions and others with tears rolling down their faces. I had been part of the latter group just the year before. I took one last, long look at the racecourse and thought about how—no matter what happened—this would be my last time running on this horse track. After doing our warm-up mile jog, I walked to our team tent where I kept my racing bag and began to prepare myself for the race that was now about thirty minutes away. I took out my racing flats, placed them on my feet, and tied the bright-green laces as tightly as I could, knot after knot. I was always made fun of for having so many knots in my laces. But, I figured, better safe than sorry. Not to mention, one of my racing flats had actually gotten stuck in the mud of a race my freshman year, and I had to finish with one bare foot.

I took my race bib number from my coach's hand as she smiled; she knew it was a special day for me. I pinned my number to my uniform and left with the rest of my team to walk to the starting line. I couldn't stop my mind from having a quick flashback to this walk, just one year ago. But the difference in my mind and heart this time around was a beautiful thing to compare. I had been so nervous and selfish last time I was here, only wanting to win out of competiveness and for my own gain. Last year I had been a nervous wreck both the night before and the day of the race because of depending on and focusing on solely myself.

But not this year. No, this year was very different. I walked to that line with confidence—not confidence in myself and not even confidence that I would win—but knowing that Christ was there along my side and that, whatever happened, life would be great. Win or lose, I had already won in my heart. I had met an amazing guy, I was truly free from my eating disorder, I was growing in my relationship with Christ more than ever before each and every day, and I had finally realized that running wasn't everything. I knew that if I won, I'd be ecstatic and give Christ all the glory. But if I didn't win, I knew I would still leave that day with a joy and thankfulness in my heart to God for bringing me as far as He already had this season, as both a runner and as a person. And it was a beautiful thing to see my friend Katie lining up on the sidelines, ready to cheer me and the rest of the team on. Just one year ago, I thought our friendship was ruined. Just one year ago, it was on this exact course that our friendship hit an all time low. But this year was different; now running for a college, restoration had come.

As we lined up on the starting line, we circled up as a team and I prayed; this would be the last time of my high school career. As I ended the prayer and got into position, I began to pray silently, saying something like this:

Father, I just thank you for all You have already done in my life. I have truly seen Your goodness, and I just feel so blessed for where You have brought me already. I know that with my strength alone, I'm capable of nothing today. But I also know that with You, I *do* have the capability of doing something great today. I'm choosing to lay everything in Your hands, and I pray that You'll be with me and guide me these next coming minutes as I run. I pray that Your strength will carry me through and allow me to run a better race than I ever could on my own. But, above all, I thank You no matter what happens today. I want Your will to be done, and that is why I will choose to be thankful and praise You, no matter what the outcome is. I love You, Jesus.

If It Were Easy, Everyone Would Do It

I already knew what it felt like to give up; so I decided I wanted to see what would happen when I didn't.

BANG! THE GUN went off, and all 181 girls sprinted away. That season, I was known to go out hard and lead the race…and I was also known to die soon after and finish miserably. But I knew I had to start off quickly again this race if I wanted to stand a chance. My competitors had a lot of talent, and I couldn't allow any extra hope to ignite the fire within them. I sprinted with all my strength up the long, uphill stretch for the first of three times during that race. Not only were my feet racing, but my mind was also racing. This was real. The race had finally come. It had finally started. I was now running my last high-school cross-country race. I had to give it all I had.

After the first quarter mile of the 3.1-mile race, I looked around me for the first time. I realized the adrenaline rush had made me zone out the first minute or so. But I had finally settled into a pace that I was hoping to maintain, and I wanted to see who was in the top pack at this point.

That is when I felt like I experienced a slight heart attack.

I realized there was no one with me other than one other single girl. I thought to myself, *Oh no, what have I gotten myself into*? Doubts and flashbacks of bad races I had run that season began filling my mind. Was I going to experience a replay of most of that season's races, where I would lead the race and then fall back and finish terribly?

But as I looked down at my hand, I knew God was with me. Maybe my own strength would fail me, but with my God and His strength, all things were possible. He would be the strength of my heart.

I certainly hadn't pictured the race going like this in my mind, but God always has a plan of His own I have come to realize. *And today, I am going to trust it,* I thought as I continued to run. I was going to have faith and run with all my heart. Some of the best runners in the pack behind me and the other girl were known for continually increasing their pace mile by mile, and they typically came from way behind the lead runners to ultimately win the race. With that in mind, I looked to my right and said to the girl with any extra energy I had, "Let's not even give them a chance; let's go!" and I increased my pace.

Mile two came around quickly. And now I was completely on my own. Throughout every state-championship race, an announcer would always keep bystanders up-to-date. It was quite a large horse track, and fans could only see part of the course, so this was necessary. Usually, the announcer would use names, continually calling out who was in the top ten places or so. But not this time. This time, all I kept hearing was "the girl in white is leading the race!"

He didn't know my name. Nobody knew my name. Why would they need to know the name of the girls who was ranked twenty-ninth?

I was now approaching the infield—the part of the course that I was known to completely die off and fall behind at—so I looked at my hand once again for reassurance. My coach found me from the inside ring that she was allowed in and began screaming my name. "Go, Sarah Grace! You got it, but you have to go *now*!" I continued encouraging myself after I passed my coach. *Come on, Sarah Grace. Not now, you can't give in now. You have led this entire race; you* **cannot** *fall back now.*

T's family friend who was at dinner the night before, a coach and a past Olympic runner himself, shouted out to me at the two-mile mark: "The pack is about fifteen seconds behind you!" I couldn't give in now. I couldn't let them catch me. It was like a cat-and-mouse situation. And I was a terrified mouse running for my life with every ounce of energy I had. With a little over a half a mile to go, T's family friend found me again and shouted, "They are eight seconds off of you! Go, Sarah Grace! Stay strong!"

The pain had now thoroughly settled in. My legs felt numb. I felt as if I couldn't push my legs any faster. I couldn't believe that I had come this far, running the entire race by myself. Was I going to give in now? Would the pack of girls, the girls that were actually expected to win this race, catch me? And worse, would they possibly even easily pass me, making me look dumb for going out so hard in the beginning?

Emotions of all kinds welled up inside of me, as I thought back to every memory that had gotten me to where I was at that moment: Memories of winning that track race my sophomore year after the heartbreaking suicide just the day before. Memories of all the times my coach had convinced me to continue running when I wanted to quit. Memories of each endless, Saturday long run, and every tortuous mile-repeat workout after a long day of class. Memories of all the people I had met through running and the relationships I had made.

As I saw the hill in sight, I knew I couldn't give up. I had a quarter mile to go. Only one more time did I have to run up this long, slowly rising hill…one more time! I had run this hill over twenty times in the past four years of running, and I only had to do it one more time. Could I muster any more energy from deep inside?

I began my last run up the dreaded, long, and now steep-feeling hill, running with all that my legs had left in them. I couldn't lose it now; I just couldn't. I looked down at my hand, and I asked God for strength. I felt like I had nothing more to give. I knew that if God didn't give me an extra wave of energy, I would indeed be passed by the pack of runners slowly catching me. It was as if I were the bait, just waiting to be consumed by the competitors who were hungry for a state- championship title.

This last stretch was lined with hundreds of people. I could hear all the shouts, all the cheers. That is when I looked over to the inside of the track. Right behind the fence, running up the hill at my pace was my neighbor, my past teammate, now graduated and a college runner. But most importantly, she was my close friend once again. She screamed, "Go, Sarah Grace! You have this! Only yards left!"

I had to finish the mission. Unexplainable feelings welled up inside of me: partly from seeing someone whom I had seen only as competition just the prior year now cheering me on, as my close friend once again, to the finish line. And, of course, partly due to the fact that the state-championship title was down to the last ten seconds of the race. I could hear cheering for the runners who were slowly catching me, specifically for one girl in particular who was favored to win. I continued to run my heart out up the rest of that hill until I crossed the finish line.

The clock read 17 minutes and 58 seconds when the girl favored to win crossed the finish line.

The clock read 17 minutes and 50 seconds when my feet had hit the line just before hers did.

God had given me the individual state-championship title.

Runners World. "State Championship Race Finish," Todd Grasley. 11/19/10.

(Left: Katie and I immediately post-race, Top Right: my Coach Kelly and I after the podium, Bottom Right: My mom and I after the race)

Impossible: A Perspective Problem

I used to let life's problems take over my mind; but now I realize that when you change the way you look at things, the things you are looking at change.

THE EMOTIONS I had crossing that finish line are indescribable. Tears welled up in my eyes. Thoughts of all of the long, tough workouts I had put in, all of the 6:00 a.m. mornings when I had gotten up earlier than my team to run with my coach, all the past races of defeat and despair, and most importantly, all of God's goodness through it all, flooded my mind.

A girl who wasn't even ranked in the top twenty, a girl who wasn't on anyone's radar to win, was now the state champion.

I couldn't believe it. God had done it. God had given me the strength to become the next state champion. The man who had interviewed me the week before quickly approached me after my feet crossed the finish line. With tears of joy streaming down my face, I made a short, yet bold, statement into the video camera as he interviewed me: "I have God to thank for it. He was my strength today."

Like the verse on my hand said, this may have been impossible for me to do, but with God, it was made possible. The impossible transformed into the possible. And it can for you too, if only you believe. But this principle goes way past running or sports in general. Whether you believe you can or can't accomplish something, you will be right. You have to believe that you can achieve more than you have before. You have to believe that you are capable. You have to believe that you are worth more than you have thought you were in the past. Whether it is a fitness goal, a career goal, an athletic goal, or a personal goal, believe that you can reach it, and put all your energy and heart into achieving it. Because, personally speaking, I know that the worst feeling is finishing, knowing that you had more left to give. At my state race the year before—at the same course—I was ranked third. Yet, I didn't even place in the top five because I didn't giving it my all, I didn't believe in myself, and I didn't find my confidence and strength in God.

Always give it all you have. Finish that race, that game, that year of work, or that difficult situation in your life. Finish proudly—proud that you gave it all you had. Life is short. We don't know how many years, weeks, days, or hours we have left. Not even tomorrow is promised. So why not live every single moment with intention and purpose? Why not put all your energy and heart into working toward your highest aspirations right *now*? I'm telling you, if you truly believe in yourself, and you give it your all, it is the most incredible, emotional, and joyful feeling you will ever feel. You will never regret it.

An article written later that day to recap the state races started with this paragraph:

If there was really one individual shocker of the day, this was it. Going into the race, no one really put Spann in the discussion for the title…or, for the most part, even top five. But Miss Sarah Grace Spann, looking strong even to the finish and kicking with all her might, won the state championship today. Dressed in all white, she flew up the final hill with a huge PR (personal record for those wondering!).

All of this made me see the reality of a verse I once read while at a low point: "Though I have fallen, I will rise. Though I sit in darkness, the LORD will be my light" (Micah 7:8).

And that He was. Even though I was in darkness for so long—from my lowest point in high school to all of the races that resulted in feelings of failure this senior year—I knew God would be my light and would bring me out of darkness. And that is exactly what He did.

A song came to my mind in the days following the race that really spoke to me. Isn't the power of music amazing? A single song can have the ability to take you back to a specific moment years ago or produce enough emotion to lead to a crying session. Well, this song fit the story of my life to a tee. To this day, it will still take me back, as I listen to it, through all the memories I've shared with you. The song is called "Mountain of God" by Third Day. I won't include all of the lyrics, but here are just a few of the lines:

> I confess from time to time
> I lose my way
> But You are always there
> To bring me back again
>
> Even though the journey's long
> And I know the road is hard
> Well, the One who's gone before me
> He will help me carry on
> After all that I've been through
> Now I realize the truth
> That I must go through the valley
> To stand upon the mountain of God

God certainly brought me out of the lowest valley and placed me upon the highest mountain peak.

His promise and call to action in 2 Corinthians 4:17–18 is one that I love:

For our light and momentary troubles are achieving for us an eternal glory that far outweighs them all. So we fix our eyes not on what is seen, but on what is unseen, since what is seen is temporary, but what is unseen is eternal.

Something that I have come to realize is that I will always face hardship and troubles in this life—some greater than others. But when compared to the glorious home that God has planned for me in heaven, all of these troubles seem so little. The problem is that I can't see His glory yet, so it is almost impossible not to focus on my problems, seeing them as colossal dilemmas in life. It's all about perspective.

One day I saw a wonderful picture of this concept and an illustration of how perspective truly is everything: I thought back to the times I have passed houses and trucks as I drove down the street. Those trucks seemed so large from my perspective in my car. But now, think of the last time you flew in an airplane. When I'm in an airplane and look at houses and trucks from above, from a *different perspective,* they seem so miniscule! All of a sudden, something happens to the scale I use to weigh their size, and things that seemed gigantic now seem microscopic.

That's why God calls me (and you!) to have faith, to focus on what I *cannot see* yet. Sometimes, my problems and situations seem larger than I can handle because I'm right next to them, right in the midst of them. But God is calling me to look at them from *a different perspective,* to look at them from a faith-based perspective, on an eternal scale.

But there is one problem with all of this. It isn't easy. It is tough. It's a new battle each day. I realize I face a question each morning I wake up: am I going to look at life through the eyes of this world or through the eyes of Jesus.

Endings Lead to New Beginnings

I used to fear anything new; but now I see there is beauty in welcoming new beginnings.

A COUPLE WEEKS after the state race, I made my final decision and officially announced that I would be running for the University of Florida. Before the state-championship race, I had thought that it would definitely be my last high-school cross-country race of the season. But because of the way things turned out, I was off to nationals up in Charlotte, North Carolina. So, two weeks after the state race, T and I went up together in a charter bus with a few other runners. He had placed well at states too; but with higher aspirations than I ever had for the race, he was disappointed upon finishing anything less than number one. Still, he was excited for this trip though and the end of cross country season; his talent and passion was on the track.

Unlike the state race though, we promised each other this last, national race was just for fun. That may sound crazy to read. I'm sure you're thinking, *What are you talking about, Sarah Grace, you didn't care about nationals?* But by this point, I had all that I needed. I was on such a high, I could have cared less about the outcome of this one. To be honest, all I was focused on was the joy of having a gold medal and the fact that I would get to spend a weekend in North Carolina with T.

Nationals always takes place the weekend after Thanksgiving. So after spending Thanksgiving with my family at my sister's house, I met the big charter bus off the highway that took all the runners up to the race who lived in my area. It was a twelve-hour ride, but it seemed extremely short—only because T was right behind me. We talked everything and got to know each other more deeply by the hour.

The guy who interviewed me before and after the state race was on our bus as well. We all became pretty friendly after a twelve-hour bus ride, and he became comfortable enough to act his comical self. Joke after joke came out of his mouth. "So, when are you going to date? Hey, T, are you going to ask her out soon?" I was embarrassed but loved the teasing at the same time.

We arrived at that town filled with beautiful mountains and autumn's fallen leaves all around. After reaching our hotel, T asked me to go on a walk outside since it was so beautiful. I quickly agreed and went to my room to change clothes. As we began our walk, I reflected on what a great guy T was. Every word that came out of his mouth was so caring. Not once was anything negative said about anyone or anything. I was also wondering if T would ask me to be his girlfriend on that walk. However, those words did not come out of his mouth.

Funny enough, though, I was so content with where we stood with one another that it didn't matter. I knew God had a special place for T in my life. I was in no rush to make things happen in my own time.

The second night up in that beautiful North Carolina city, we decided to spend some time together again. And we did have the conversation I had hoped for that night. Although I can't tell you exactly what was said, I do know that as my heart began beating quickly, T asked me to officially be his girlfriend. And on November 26, 2010, a very special relationship began. As we drove back to our hometowns on that charter bus, I couldn't have been happier. *Everything was just right in the world.*

And the race? It went just as great as my mind-set was about it. I ran well, not my worst but not my best. On the national scale, I didn't make the top ten, which would have advanced me to another race, but I still medaled. Yet, I finished excited and ready to greet T at the finish line of his race. He also took the race more lightly. Even though not running bad by any means, he didn't place in the top ten either but medaled as well. The most freeing part was the fact that we finished excited, because it meant we were able to spend the rest of the trip free of stress, free of running, and most importantly, together. Oh, how the mentality had shifted.

The very next weekend, we ended up running yet another race, the Florida Senior All-Star Race. This was an incredibly fun race up in Tallahassee, because it was only for all the seniors. They grouped all the seniors into four teams based on location within the state. So naturally, T and I were on the same team – for once. We were wearing the same uniform for the first time, but this wouldn't be the last time. This was also a special weekend, but not because of the race itself. This weekend, T's parents and my mom and I all decided to make the six-hour drive up together. This was the first time all of us spent time together, and I couldn't have felt more contentment the entire ride up and back. Our parents were getting along so perfectly – things couldn't have felt more right. T ended up winning first out of the guys; I came in second for the girls. I remember posting a photo on social media with him and his trophy that day saying, "my champion". I could have cared less at that moment that I had lost by a few seconds, getting outkicked by the same girl I had beat at the state race just two weeks prior. Life was good.

This was definitely the start of something new—and this new beginning was something beautiful.

Journal Entry: 12/05/10

It's been awhile since I've written, but I'm still keeping up with getting in the Word daily. Since last time I wrote, I went to Nationals, ran 18:08 (felt fine about race despite not being in the top), and then went to Tallahassee with my mom, T, and his parents for the All-Star Meet! I feel like I've gotten so close to him lately. I've never liked someone this much in my entire life. I almost feel like I love him already. But I want to remain focused on God and simply thanking Him for bringing T into my life; I never want to lose him. Our parents are so close already, everything just seems perfect! Oh and ps: I committed to the University of Florida! I just know it was the right decision. And it doesn't hurt that T also signed there ☺

A Still, Small Voice

———— ⁓⊗⊘⁓ ————

I used to love reading about others' personal journeys and inspiring feats; but I never thought people would want to read mine.

As THE WEEKS passed, T and I became closer than I ever thought we would—more specifically, closer than I thought I would ever let someone get to my heart. For so long I had shut down to letting anyone in. I had felt that people in my past had failed me and had only caused me hurt. So why let someone in again? Especially a guy. With experiencing such hurt from my earthly father, I realized I subconsciously shut down to almost all men, without reason. I believed they would cause similar pain. So, without ever giving any man a chance to prove me wrong, I instantly felt distrust, shutting down completely. But this was different. Somehow, without conscious choice, my heart opened up again and made a spot for someone new.

From the beginning, we centered our entire relationship on Christ, and it made all the difference. And the best part was that—unlike any other relationship I had ever been in with a guy—it wasn't physicality that intensified the closeness I felt with him. No, it was simply T's heart and the way he treated me and everybody around him each and every day. The priorities of our relationship and our lives individually matched up: Christ number one, then our families, and our relationship with each other only after that.

From the first time I met them, T's family was loving and caring toward me. His dad became the father figure in my life I had been missing for so long. I went to him about everything that was on my heart, with full trust that he would not simply tell me what I wanted to hear, but give me the wise advice I needed to hear. T's parents were such a blessing in my life from the start. And as the days went by, they began treating me like their own daughter, showing me more love than I could have imagined possible from a family other than my own.

But the most exciting part was not that I was growing closer to T each and every day, but my relationship with the Lord was growing stronger and stronger each day. I began to crave time in His Word every morning I woke up, and I found myself spending more time seeking His desire for my life in prayer, simply because I trusted He knew best. He became a best friend to me; one that I talked to about everything, even the small, silly aspects of my life.

During one of my quiet times with the Lord, I felt Him telling me something—something big. I spent time listening and seeking with all my heart what He was trying to tell me. Then I heard Him telling me I had a story to tell. Yes, it may be a story filled with despair, sadness, and defeat. But it was also a story that finished on a high note full of hope, love, triumph, and most importantly, God's power and love. I didn't want to tell anyone about this feeling, in case I failed to follow through; but I finally opened up to T's father. His support and encouragement about this huge calling I felt deep inside my heart, is what pushed me to take the initial steps.

I knew I had a story to share.

To Remember or Not to Remember

I used to be ashamed of my past, striving to forget it all; but now I see there is beauty in remembering it.

I KNEW GOD was calling me to share my story—*this* story. But I didn't know quite how He wanted me to share it. I approached my youth leader's wife, who had been a mentor to me that year, and told her that I felt led to tell my testimony. She said she thought it would be a wonderful idea for me to share it in front of our entire youth group on parents' night the coming week. *Yes, that must be what God was trying to tell me. He wanted me to tell my story to my youth group,* I thought.

My mentor was so excited for me and couldn't wait to hear my story herself. She suggested, though, that I keep it under ten minutes, since, she said, that is how testimonies are most effective to a young crowd. I guess a thing called "attention span" is a huge factor.

I began writing my thoughts, as I began to sort out what I wanted to share. I kept trying to limit myself and only include the biggest events and most important details. I ended up not have ten minutes worth of writing to share, but ten pages! I had no idea how I would cut it down to the time constraint given. But in my struggle to do so, I came across something that made my stomach do a million flips inside of me. I began searching through old documents I had saved on my computer, looking for Bible verses I had come across throughout the years; I would save Word documents full of them in my times of struggle. I came across something from my past—something absolutely incredible, something that sent goose bumps all up and down my body. It was an old document, a document labeled "Sarah Grace's Desires." My jaw dropped as I opened the document and read what was in it.

Sarah Grace's Desires
1. Complete healing of anorexia: internal, external, and outside relationships
2. A best friend: whom I can walk with and grow in Christ with
3. A guy: who will truly love me for who I am, has eyes for no one else, and loves Christ over all things
4. A state-championship title in cross-country in 2009

Remember that document I wrote way back in the beginning of high school, when my mom told me I needed to write down what I was asking God for in my life? Well, I had forgotten about it a long time ago. But God hadn't. And He had given me every single thing I had asked for.

I had overcome my inner battle with food, no longer using it as a source of control. I was not only at a healthy weight, but I was at a healthy state of mind now.

I not only had found one Jesus-loving close friend in the past year but *three*, who inspired me each day in my walk with the Lord. (One was, Emily, the girl who sat behind me in math class my junior year and was always asking me to go to youth group with her. And yes, we are still close friends today!)

And I most certainly found a guy who loved me for being simply Sarah Grace, not someone I wasn't, like guys had in the past. It was the most refreshing feeling in the world. Plus, I had not only found a guy who loved me but who loved the Lord with all of his heart. Talk about restoring my hope for the male race!

And, lastly, I may not have won the state championship in 2009, but I certainly did in 2010. God knew I wasn't ready in 2009 for something like that. I was stuck in self-pride and unhealthy competitiveness. I would have taken all the credit myself, and because I was expected to be in the top, others would have given me the credit too. I had growing and maturing to do before I was ready to be taken to the mountaintop. And God knew that. God's plans are always greater than mine, and He granted my prayer in *His* time, not mine. He answered my prayer when He knew I was ready for it mentally and spiritually and when it would be clear as day—not only to me but to every other person who watched or heard about it—that it was His strength and not mine. I had no chance to win on my own; I was in a season of weakness. And I've come to realize that is exactly when He loves to show His power.

I didn't know how to react. Once again, God had completely amazed me with His greatness, power, and goodness.

No Better Moment than the Present

I used to think I needed to wait until I was ready; but now I realize if I wait until I'm ready, I'll be waiting for the rest of my life.

I DID TELL my testimony at church that next week, as my mentor had suggested, in front of all the high-school students and their parents. I felt so overwhelmed with joy as I remembered the journey God had brought me through, and I also felt joyful knowing that I had listened to Him and "told the story I had been given to share." I was overcome by such happiness that I was able to share without embarrassment, how my times of struggle and weakness had made me stronger in the end. My story had refined me, shaped me, and strengthened me into the girl God desired me to be, a better version of Sarah Grace. Not only did I walk away overwhelmed with joy, but it was received better than I could have ever imagined. Both parents and students approached me, immediately that night and for weeks to come, telling me how proud they were of me, sharing how much my story had impacted them, or voicing their desire for the same freedom I had come to discover myself. I was speechless by the response. *My story might actually be helpful to people?* That question in my mind became more clear as I continued to receive positive feedback.

Soon after that night I told my testimony, I heard God's voice once again in my quiet time. I felt Him telling me once again that I had a story to tell and that I needed to tell it.

I was puzzled. I thought I had done that by sharing my testimony at church. *Didn't I already do that, God?* I didn't know what He could mean. But there is a truth I have now come to understand. God says in Isaiah 55:8, "For my thoughts are not your thoughts, neither are your ways my ways." One thing is certain. His plans were far greater than mine. They were much greater than I could have ever imagined, and they always will be.

God was calling me to write a book.

It didn't happen overnight. It didn't even happen within the next year. I disregarded the earlier impression Christ had made on my heart, as I reasoned things out in my head: I was too busy writing this paper and that paper in order to finish off my senior year strong; I would do it after graduation, during the summer. But soon, I became too busy once again—now, with getting ready for college. Which is why, I did not do what I had felt the Lord calling me to do until *after college*. One quick lesson, if you think you'll be less busy in your future, you are wrong. Life is crazy, and it never stops getting more demanding as you go.

Once again—in the middle of my master's program and dietetic internship, and through a series of events that couldn't have been by chance—I felt the need to do what I knew I had been called to do.

One night I was talking to my roommate about some of my past experiences and both what I had learned and the ways I had grown from them. She made a comment that I will never forget: "Sarah Grace, you need to write a book!" *What? I had never told her, or almost anyone, about this calling I had felt to write a book. Where was this coming from?*

That very still, small voice of the Lord was reminding me again of what He had placed on my heart to do years ago.

I still had a story to tell. And this time I would listen. I would listen, and I would write.

There is no better moment than the present to do what you feel called to do.

Peace that Passes All Understanding

I used to think being a Christian meant I got immunity from difficulties; but now I realize it simply means I get peace in the midst of them.

So I FINALLY listened, and I finally began writing. Now, as I write, I am currently a graduate student pursuing my master's in sports nutrition, while also completing my dietetic internship—oh, and running a little blog and Instagram (Fresh Fit N Healthy) that I created in undergrad (part two of my story? Just kidding…). I'm also still trying to live a normal life by spending time with people, living an active life doing things that I love, and simply making *me* time. And I can verify that life never gets less busy. (And as a side note: even though this may come as a surprise, I barely run anymore. I've actually picked up weight training to stay fit, with the occasional run when I have a lot on my mind.) Anyways, back to what I was saying. There is never a time you will feel ready to take on a big project or set off to accomplish a huge goal. There will never be a perfect moment when you have all the free time in the world to accomplish something. I've come to appreciate Nike and the company's slogan "just do it" because it has become my life motto.

In my life's journey, since that state race my senior year of high school, I have come to learn some things.

Disclaimer before sharing these lessons: My life is far from perfect. I am far from perfect. I still make mistakes. I still let my weaknesses win some times, and I still feel as if I've failed often. But that's the beautiful thing. I'm human. You are human. We are going to mess up. We are not going to be perfect. And *that's okay*. What isn't okay is not getting back up once you fall. What isn't okay is not trying again after failing the last one hundred times. What isn't okay is beating yourself up and losing hope in yourself.

Every day is a new day—a new day to make the changes you want to see in your life.

As I continue to live this journey of mine hand in hand with Jesus, I've come to realize one very important thing: life isn't easy. Following Jesus doesn't mean all your problems just disappear. If you're living to your potential, pursuing constant growth and the path you're meant to walk, it won't be easy. There will be days you want to give in, days you want to give up, days you simply just want to break down and scream, "Why?" So I never want to portray a picture that my life, or any life, is problem-free and temptation-free after choosing to pursue a relationship with Jesus. I know I have many days where I just break down in tears, sometimes over silly things, sometimes over things that deserve the waterworks. But no matter the cause of them, I share in order to let you in on the truth that my life is not always happy-go-lucky, as most on social media try to portray these days.

Have you ever bought something, only to feel like the advertisement you saw for it painted a false picture of how it truly works (or doesn't work)? Or think about social media as an example as I briefly just mentioned above, as that is probably the worst culprit in our generation of portraying things as they aren't. You think others' lives are simply *perfect* because of comparing your behind-the-scenes to their highlight reel that they choose to share on social media. (In case you didn't realize it, people don't tend to share all the not-so-glorious minutes, hours, and days in between the highlights).

Sometimes, I feel the American church tends to paint a similar, false picture. You sign up to follow Jesus based on a false depiction that becoming a Christian means you will never have a another problem or a temptation to do the wrong thing again. But then you begin experiencing the same temptations and problems as before, and you find yourself feeling frustrated and let down. Have you felt that way already? I know I did. I asked the question "why?" every single day of my senior year in high school. Why was I still struggling in my races? Why was I still having temptations to control my food when things didn't go as planned? Why did I still have problems after choosing to follow Jesus?

Satan is alive and real, and he is looking for any way he can to take down those living for Christ. I used to compare myself to my old friends, wondering, *Why am I struggling so much and having these bad things happen when I am doing all the right things and they aren't?* Of course, I wasn't perfect; actually I was no better then any of them on God's scale, but this was my mindset.

But it all makes sense now. As an athlete, I like seeing it this way:

Think about heading out on the field or court to start a game. Are you going to guard and try to spoil the efforts of the player on the other team who has zero ability to score and isn't a threat to your plan of winning, or are you going to focus on the player that is known for having amazing athletic capabilities —the one who will actually make a huge difference in the game?

Satan is not dumb. Why waste his time pursuing someone who isn't going to impact the game (life on earth)? Why spend his energy tempting someone and causing problems in someone's life who isn't hurting his cause?

He wants to use his energy to prevent the works of those who are making an impact—those who are living for Christ.

And, unfortunately, he will try to use your greatest weaknesses against you. But with that "unfortunately," there is good news too. We may have Satan coming against us, but we have a God who is much more powerful *for* us—and is on our side.

Have I recovered from my past issues with anorexia? Yes. But will this always be an area of weakness for me? Yes. And I must make sure I am diligently seeking God to keep from straying away and allowing Satan to defeat me through my weaknesses. I will always have struggles in life, whether that is wanting to control my food or something completely different. But now, with Jesus, I can have peace and strength in the midst of my trials and come out as a conqueror.

I've come to realize that I am weak (and not just physically). I have come to realize that I will be overcome if I try to stand on my own, and I will fall back into old weaknesses and temptations if I try to succeed on my own. But with God's strength, I can stand strong. This is why, as a follower of Jesus, I must continually pray for self-control, discernment, vision, strength, help, and clarity as I read His word. Every single day, I am in need of Jesus and His word to have strength for that specific day. His word isn't cake for special occasions. It's called our daily bread for a reason. As a soon-to-be registered dietitian, I can appreciate this analogy in knowing the importance of fueling our bodies with food for energy and strength throughout the day.

Each day is about choices, and every day I have two: I can either choose to follow Christ, living for Him and trusting *in* Him and His strength. Or, I can choose to follow the world, being overcome by negative thoughts and dangerous tendencies.

Will I ever be perfect? Not even close. Will I have a problem-free life? No. I still have, and always will have, struggles in life. Whether it be low times of desperation, frustration, anxiety, or sadness, or times of temptation to resort to old habits, difficulties will come up in life.

But I learned a lesson one day from my pastor that I took to heart: "Don't let your reality define you." We cannot let our struggles define who we are. We cannot let our weaknesses define who we are. We must allow Christ to define who we are.

How does *He* define us? He says that we are "created…in *His own* image" (Genesis 1:27) and that we are "fearfully and wonderfully made" (Psalm 139:14). And that alone can give us hope and confidence, even in the darkest moments. *He* will give us strength and peace, no matter what we are going through.

I can choose to trust or to defy.

I can choose to trust and have peace in the midst of difficulties, or I can choose to defy and continue to struggle. I can choose to let Jesus use my difficulties for my good, or I can choose to allow those same difficulties to be a stumbling block that I fall over.

And it's not a choice we make once. This is a choice we make several times every day.

My advice is this: choose the peace that passes all of our understanding.

There is Freedom in Surrender

I used to think that if only I tried harder, I would gain control over my struggles and overcome; but now I realize the only way to experience victory is to ask for help.

JUST THE OTHER day, a wrestler in the nutrition office where I volunteer was talking about a match he lost. He told me he should have been awarded points, but the ref said that he wasn't in control (a rule in wrestling), despite having the other guy on the floor. This wrestler thought he was in control and succeeding, only to be told his perception was an illusion.

That story stuck with me all afternoon.

I like to be in control. As you've read, desiring to have control in life is a specialty of mine; it's what led to my eating disorder. But as I continued to think about this wrestler's story, I couldn't help but to relate it back to my own life.

How many times have I found myself wrestling with a problem, trying to overcome it (and believing I was getting somewhere) on my own? I can just see Jesus sitting up in heaven, watching me wrestle under this false illusion that I have everything under control, just waiting for me to surrender my own efforts and ask Him for help.

I always think I'll succeed if only I try harder or if only I find the perfect system to manage my time so that I can accomplish everything I want to do. If only I put all my heart and soul into something, I can do it. *I'm independent. I don't need anyone else. I've got this.* I tend to think I can be in control and overcome any problem in my life.

But the truth is, that sense of being in control is just a false illusion. Just like the ref told that wrestler, Jesus is constantly telling me, "You aren't in control; you aren't winning this battle." The only way I can truly have victory over my problems and overcome my greatest struggles is to daily admit I *don't* have control over them and then ask Jesus for His help to overcome.

In my past, despite all the other issues going on that I didn't have control over, restricting my food gave me a false illusion that I was in control. I thought I was winning the battles I was experiencing every day in my family life, academic life, and personal life…because of a false illusion of being in control through my food intake.

But Jesus was sitting up in heaven telling me I wasn't in control. He was telling me I was not winning by restricting my food. He was waiting patiently for me to realize the truth, to reach out my hands, and to ask for help. And the moment I realized I didn't have control, the moment that I realized I needed help…He immediately reached down His hand to rescue me. I rose from the valley of despair as a conqueror because I surrendered the fight to gain control, and simply asked for help.

Life will never be perfect. Life will always be filled with struggles, temptations, and unexpected valleys.

But I have come to realize I *can* overcome; I just need God's help. And you can overcome too.

Unlocking Your Freedom

I used to think freedom was found in having power to break the chains; but now I realize it's much easier to surrender and simply ask Jesus for the keys to unlock them.

THE TRUTH I'VE touched on earlier, of life never being perfect, even after overcoming one struggle or valley, was evident my senior year in high school. My life was far from perfect after reaching the mountaintop of becoming a state champion.

The very next month after that state race, I experienced a knee injury that would prevent me from running my entire senior-year track season. During this last spring semester of my high school running career, I once again felt overwhelmed with sadness and frustration. *What is happening God?! I thought I had come out of my valleys for good! Haven't I suffered enough? I'm trying to do good for your name by using running as a platform, and now it's being taken away?!* Some of the deep despair I felt during this time has left my mind now, but looking back through old journal entries, it all comes back quite easily and vividly. Almost every entry during this period mentioned the pain.

Here are just a few of my thoughts during this time period:

Journal Entry: 1/17/11
"I have learned the secret of being content in any and every situation"
(Philippians 4:12)

This was good for me to remember, as my knee has been hurting and I had to take the whole weekend off! I was hoping it would feel all better today, but it didn't. I get so down because I hate not being able to run, but this verse helped me to see I need to be content no matter what is happening...

Journal Entry: 1/31/11
"But rejoice inasmuch as you participate in the sufferings of Christ" (1 Peter 4:13)
        This verse really spoke to me today, because now it is going on three weeks of not running, and T's coach/mentor told me I should expect to be out the entire season. The MRI showed no torn ligaments or tendons, but just a notch under my knee cap that is probably causing the pain. But anyways, I still can't run, and I constantly have to fight the sadness away. It's a daily struggle, but God's really been showing me so much. I feel ashamed for being so upset about just one thing being taken from my life. It shows me I'm probably putting running too high in my life. But, I will just continue laying my hands on my knee and praying over it, hoping that Jesus heals me.
        "Be joyful in hope, patient in affliction, faithful in prayer" (Romans 12:12)

Journal Entry: 2/09/11
"For it is God who works in you" (Philippians 2:13)

This is the verse that stood out to me today in my reading, because I got a bad report from the doctor yesterday and was extremely upset. The doctor said this whole knee pain "has to work itself out" and that it "could be weeks, could be years" before I can run pain-free again. I let myself get so down, thinking everything with UF was going to be messed up now. But I need to remember my God is bigger than any doctor's report or pain. This situation is really teaching me how to fully rely on God and not myself. I just need to keep my head up and pray!

Journal Entry: 2/10/11
"For truly I tell you, until heaven and earth disappear, not the smallest letter, not the least stroke of a pen, will by any means disappear from the Law until everything is accomplished."
(Matthew 5:18)

This is so reassuring in that every promise of God will stand true. I realize I just need to have full faith in Him through this time. Today was SUCH a better day! I went to physical therapy and they gave me hope! At least something is being done now. Then I brought T to my youth group for the first time tonight, and he loved it and said he wanted to come next week! It makes me so happy. Today was such a good day. God is good. I need to remember days like this when I'm struggling.

Journal Entry: 2/23/11
I began reading Deuteronomy 28 today, and all about the blessings for obedience. But then I came across the curses for disobedience. This just burdened my heart so much, because I don't feel like it was by chance I was led to read this chapter today in the Bible. I feel like God is trying to open my eyes to all the "weeds" in my life that are choking me. I know I need to obey my parents more, because lately my mom and I have been fighting nonstop. She even told me I should just move out the other day. And for my dad, no matter how much he has hurt me in the past, I realize that cutting off all

communication with him is not being respectful. He is my father no matter what and I need to try to start talking to him again. I also realized that the other major thing in my life is not honoring the Sabbath and resting on Sunday. I always make myself run, and I need to trust God and just take that day off, giving my body the rest that it needs. Just some thoughts this morning!

Journal Entry: 3/20/11
"A prayer of an afflicted person who has grown weak and pours out a lament before the Lord. Hear my prayer, Lord; let my cry for help come to You." (Psalm 102:1)

   This is me today. It's now been months since I have been able to run. And things aren't looking up. Track season is halfway through, and at this point, there is no way I will compete at all this season. I guess I need to just stop questioning what I did to deserve having running taken from me. I really thought I was on the right track finally with giving all the glory to Him and even giving my testimony in church at youth group. And I know God uses all things for the good, and that He has a plan to prosper me and not to harm me, but this situation just makes me feel so hopeless. It's so hard to believe those promises of God when you're in a valley. I just don't understand why this is happening, especially as soon as I sign with a college and begin getting excited for my future in it. What if it's not God's Will for me to run in college? That makes me so sad to think about! I know I need to accept that joyfully if so, but the thought of not running anymore makes me SO SAD. But deep, DEEP down, I know it is God who I need to find my complete joy and happiness in, and not anything of this world. Ugh, life is tough! This journey as a Christian isn't easy!

As you can see, my life was a roller-coaster during this season. Some days I felt hope, but more days than others, I felt total despair as I questioned God's goodness. But I realized I couldn't let that knee injury define me or my happiness. Despite there being days when I was more tempted then others to let my injury define me, I didn't let it steal my joy.

I still strive to not allow my problems to define me. It's not always the easiest decision, but I choose to trust and allow Jesus to use my problems for my good and to refine me as a person, rather than letting them be a stumbling block that I fall over and feel hopeless or defiant about.

This isn't something that comes naturally. It never will. It is a choice we have to choose each day. But to let Jesus take the burden of your difficulties is a choice that is so worth it.

I learned that a life with Jesus at the wheel is a life filled with a joy and hope that I would not otherwise have. It offers a joy that does not fade. I realized that no matter what I was going through, or that I continue to go through, Jesus was and always will be on my side fighting. I wasn't alone then, and I will never be alone as I walk forward.

For a long while, I wondered what James 1:2–3 was talking about:

"Consider it pure joy, my brothers and sisters, whenever you face trials of many kinds, because you know that the testing of your faith produces perseverance. Let perseverance finish its work so that you may be mature and complete, not lacking anything."

Consider it joy when I'm suffering? In the past, I couldn't wrap my mind around this statement. But it makes so much sense now that I have a personal relationship with Christ. God isn't calling us to be joyful *about* our present circumstances, but He is calling us to remember. We must remember what eternal glory we have awaiting us (a.k.a, heaven!), and find hope in both that and in the fact that this current struggle is shaping us into who God desires us to be.

He will use all that we go through for our good. Even when we can't fathom how the circumstance we are going through could ever be turned into something for our good, we can have hope. It isn't the easy times in life that make us strong. It isn't in the calm that we grow as individuals. No, it is the times of struggle and conflict that strengthen us and allow us to grow. These verses that once seemed so Bible-ish and unpractical now feel alive and true.

Yes, I may have gone through some enormous struggles and very low valleys. And if you are human, you probably have too. We all do. But all of it—all of my times of despair, tears, loss, and great hardship—all of it was developing me into *God's "perfect and complete" Sarah Grace.* "Now I realize the truth, that I must go through the valley, to stand upon the mountain of God" (Third Day).

I had overcome. I had overcome my family and friendship complications and had found restoration in many of my relationships, including my dad. Yes, someone I would not even speak to, I was now speaking weekly to on the phone and going out to dinner with occasionally. I had overcome my negative mind-set about my body and food, and was now feeding and treating my body as a temple. I had overcome my lack of confidence and replaced the insecurity with courage and confidence. I had overcome my fears of failure, learning to step out of my comfort zone. I had overcome that state race my senior year and the struggles I had experienced all season leading up to it. I had overcome my dark past as a whole. I was no longer a slave to my low self-esteem, to my family issues, to my need for control, or to my eating disorder...I was a conqueror.

For the longest time, I had felt a need to find control in my life because I thought that would offer me freedom. But I couldn't have been more wrong. For so long I felt I needed to gain control to overcome and succeed. But, again, I was wrong.

All those years of trying to gain some sort of control through restricting my food only added more chains that weighed me down—chains of anger, bitterness, depression, jealousy, and self-destruction.

And it was only because of Jesus unlocking all of those chains that I was able to feel free at last. He had given me the keys to unlock my freedom. He was waiting with the keys the entire time, eagerly waiting for me to seek *freedom* by seeking Him. But He waited patiently for me to ask for the keys and desire the freedom myself. We don't have because we don't ask. And He continues to wait for us to seek Him, each day of our lives, ready to offer His strength, His comfort, and His peace.

He wants nothing more than to see us overcome and be victors.

I finally realized that nothing except Jesus would offer me the keys to unlock my freedom. The world had told me that being in control of my own life was the key to success. But the world had lied to me. Everything else and everyone else had failed me. And until I turned over all control to Jesus—laying all my worries, preoccupations, and sinful habits at His feet—I would never feel free.

I can now say I feel released—free from all of my past, all of my issues, all of my faults, all of the times I have screwed up. And you can be released from your past too. You can be a conqueror. With God's help, you can unlock your freedom. This isn't to say that things haven't come up since in my life, that have tried to chain me back down. But now, I can walk in the truth of God's faithfulness. No, my journey hasn't been perfect since trusting in God, and I definitely have had doubts at times still when choosing to follow where He is guiding me. There have been many times since that I have second guessed God's goodness and wanted to follow my plan instead of His. But that is the beauty of it all. He never gives up on us. He is always right by our side waiting to reach out His hand when we come to our senses again and realize He is the only one that offers freedom and authentic joy.

Tears came to my eyes as I thought about all the ways Jesus has stood by my side, never letting me down despite my inconsistency. We are stuck in a continually changing world, with people who are always inconsistent and will let us down at one time or another. But not Jesus. No matter how far I ran, no matter how much I mocked Him and basically spit in his face by slowly destroying the beautiful body He created and pursuing a lifestyle without Him that I thought would fulfill me…He never left me. He had compassion on me. He continued to pursue me. He turned the ashes I had created into something beautiful, like He promises to do. He waited patiently for me to offer me freedom. And His arms were wide open when I finally looked His way and found Him eagerly awaiting to embrace me with His comfort and peace.

He will do the same thing for you. He will continue to pursue you. He will turn your ashes into beauty. He will free you from whatever is weighing you down. He will use your greatest difficulties and screw-ups for your good. He will turn what was meant to destroy you around, and He will use it to refine you and mold you into the person you were created to be.

You have never gone too far. You have never messed up too much. He loved us at our worst, even dying for us—"But God demonstrates his own love for us in this: While we were still sinners, Christ died for us" (Romans 5:8)—and He will continue to love us and show us grace. He will continue to pursue us even when we make the same mistakes again. It's a relentless pursuit. And I couldn't be more thankful that He was relentless in His pursuit of me, not giving up on me even in my worst moments, because I wouldn't be where I am today if He had.

We will never be perfect, and He knows that. But Jesus looks at our hearts. As long as we are continually choosing daily to follow Him, looking to Him for strength and direction, He will continue to help us.

It is a process that never ends. It is a constant journey of being refined and being matured into who we are meant to be. It is a constant journey of learning to trust Him instead of defy Him when we are struggling. It is a constant journey that will never be perfected.

But when we are striving to be the best we can be—when I am striving to be the best Sarah Grace I can be—we can rest assure that He will be pleased.

We can know without a doubt that He will remain right by our side in our darkest moments.

We can know without a doubt that He will help us reach our potential in this life.

We can know without a doubt that He will turn victims into victors.

We can know without a doubt that He will turn our ashes into beauty.

We can know without a doubt that He will break our chains.

We can know without a doubt that He will unlock our freedom.

We can know without a doubt that He will give us victory.

As soon as we ask, we can know without a doubt that He will help us overcome.

The Cycle of an Imperfect Life

I used to believe that once I arrived on the mountain top as a conqueror, my spot there was secure; but now I see life will have endless valleys and mountain tops.

I SO BADLY wanted to end this book at my state race, when I was on the mountain top and everything seemed to be smooth-sailing and picture perfect. But as I began editing my last draft, I knew I needed to include a last chapter of some of the not-so-perfect, lower moments in my life since that state race.

Throughout that spring semester of senior year, I continued to struggle with knee pain, and finally had to surrender any hope of running that last high school track season. As you saw in journal entries, this was anything but easy. One day I would wake up positive, knowing God had a plan in it. The next, I would feel nothing but despair and hopelessness. I would swim in my neighborhood's lake for about an hour almost every day in attempts to stay somewhat in shape, which was nothing but complete misery. On a positive note, T and I became more close each and every day, sharing special moments in life together like his high school prom, Easter, our graduation ceremonies, and in our excitement over signing with the University of Florida as a soon-to-be D1 student-athletes. We also were growing closer to Christ individually and as a couple, which offered us both a joy that no hardship could take away. Oh, and even though T may not have won states in cross country, he did end up winning the state title in the mile that spring. I was so proud of him; yet, I would be lying if I said it wasn't a struggle to not let my inability to run bother me as I cheered him on. But deep down, I really was genuinely so happy for him. He deserved it.

As spring semester came to a close, my knee pain dwindled with no rhyme or reason, and I was able to slowly but surely begin to start training again. It was just around this time that sign-ups for a summer senior mission trip to Haiti were due for my church. Earlier in fall, I was ecstatic about this trip and all I would gain from such an incredible experience. However, now all I could think was, *this means another two weeks of training I have to give up. I can't afford that now. I'm just getting back into shape. I need to be at my fullest potential by the time I get to UF in August.*

Thankfully, my youth pastor's wife that had been mentoring me opened my eyes as to how selfish that thinking of mine was. Those thoughts unveiled my heart and how I was putting running before God. I signed up for the mission trip, despite still having some apprehension. Looking back, it was the best decision I had ever made. By the end of the trip, I had experienced such a shift in perspective. I saw how blessed I was, and it made me realize how often I become discontent over silly, little things. I could share some of the hundreds of photos I took, or a few of the many stories I wrote in my journal throughout the trip, but no photo or story would do justice in conveying my experience. It is one of those experiences you have to witness for yourself. But in all, I came back with a fresh and new perspective, feeling as if I had made strides in my spiritual growth during those two weeks in Haiti. And funny enough, I felt like I was still in great shape despite taking an extra two weeks off.

Isn't it funny how things work out for the best when you surrender your plans and follow God's? I am so thankful for mentors in my life, whether it be my youth pastor's wife or others like my running coach who were all part of the process in strengthening, maturing and refining me.

I was feeling fresh. I was feeling fit. But most importantly, I was feeling *free*. I was ready to begin the new chapter in my life called "college."

But once again as often happens in this roller-coaster ride called life, some twists, turns, and unexpected plunges occurred throughout these next four years of college.

In all honestly, that is life for you. Life is just that, a roller-coaster. You will constantly be thrown for unexpected highs and unpredicted lows throughout your different chapters of life. There is a season for everything, some seasons you'll be more thankful for than others. But that my friends, is the beauty in it all. If life was predictable and perfect – if our life was smooth-sailing and not a day went by where there was some uncertainty or struggle, we would be completely independent. We would have no need for a God.

And even though there is a time and place for living in a perfect world – heaven—right now we live in a flawed, crazy world. A world where we need a God that is bigger and better than us. A God that is all-knowing. A God that is a good and has our best intentions in mind. A God that remains the same in this ever-changing world. Thankfully, we have a God who is all of those things and more to walk through this life with.

After signing with the University of Florida, having the support of both T and God daily in my life, and having just experienced the trip of a lifetime in Haiti, I thought I was ready to conquer the world as I headed up to Gainesville.

But soon enough as I began those eighty mile running weeks of training, my knee pain suddenly resurrected from what I had hoped was gone forever. That first semester of college, I was in and out of the training room. I always walked in with hope that they would figure it out, and always left with despair, coming to the realization this problem may never be completely cured. Through the hours of cross training in the pool to maintain my endurance, many shed tears on the phone with my mom and my close friends Emily and Katie, and an unexplainable sense down deep in my heart that this was no longer right for my life, unhappiness, emptiness, and questioning began filling my heart. Leaving my dorm at 5:30am for practice, then having to go straight from the locker-room to class until 3pm, then coming back to the track for my second run, then going to the weight room until about 5:30pm, and then finally at last, getting back to my dorm for the first time around 6pm, was a typical day for me. I would get back exhausted, starving, and anxious about all the homework I had to finish, only to get into bed and have to do it all over again. This is what led to feeling stressed, upset and unfulfilled each night. Many nights I couldn't even sleep out of anxiety and exhaustion. I had no time to think, no time to get involved in other places on campus, no time for new friendships or to invest in current ones, and most importantly, no time for myself and my own health. Unfortunately, during this time of despair, I initially began losing weight again; but I was able to catch it and get it under control before it went too far.

I came back that spring semester after Christmas break, running again, at a healthy weight again, and yet, still unhappy and full of uncertainty that this was right for my life any longer. And that scared me more than ever. Running was my life. Running was my friend group. Running was where my talent was. Running was my platform for sharing God with others. And sadly, it had subconsciously become my identity as well. I came to college with the mindset that nothing but Jesus would ever define me; yet, at the thought of letting running go from my life completely, I was overcome with fear and anxiety. People knew me in college as Sarah Grace, the runner. I thought I would be seen as a quitter. I wondered if I was truly being called to walk away, or whether I was being called to stick it through this rough patch. I questioned whether I would ever know what the "right" decision was, or if I needed to step out in faith and trust that these feelings deep inside of me were from Jesus. *What if people just thought I was being weak and throwing away talent because it wasn't easy? What if people thought of me as a quitter?*

After many talks with close friends and mentors whom I trusted, along with many hours in prayer with the One who knows all, I made the tough decision to walk away from being a student-athlete for the University of Florida that summer after freshman year. It was one of the most difficult decisions I had ever made. But, I had to finally be honest with myself. Running was no longer growing me as a person, it was no longer serving a positive role in my life, and it was no longer making me happy. In the realization of those three things, I knew it was the healthiest decision for my life to walk away.

Do you feel stuck? Are you doubting whether something or someone is meant to remain in your life? Let me offer some advice I took myself: if something is no longer growing you, serving you, or making you happy, it is time to walk away. No matter how hard it may be at first, it is the right decision. No change is easy. Entering a new season will never be comfortable. But listening to that voice of reason deep inside of you, will never let you down or lead you astray.

My story is proof of that.

You may wonder if I questioned whether running that first year was a mistake or a waste of time? If I had just never signed with UF, and went to college as a normal student, would I have made the "better choice". If I could do it again, would I not choose to run at all in college? And I would confidently tell you no. Because of being an athlete that first year, I gained an experience I would have never wanted to miss. I was able to have impact on the people around me. I was able to grow through the pain and despair I felt each and every day, as it made me seek Jesus more than ever. And probably the most incredible outcome of that year looking back, was that working with a sports dietitian myself as an athlete, made me realize that was exactly what I wanted to do in life. That was my calling – becoming a registered dietitian.

I quickly changed my major of international relations and plans of going to law school, to a terrifying, science major of food science and human nutrition, with plans on becoming a registered dietitian and working with athletes. Like I said, God's plans are always greater than ours; even though it's not always easy after that realization to trust and have faith when life takes future twists and turns. It's a daily decision to trust and walk hand in hand with our God, having faith that He is good and has a plan to prosper us, not to harm us.

In all my free time of no longer getting up at 5:30am and being out and busy until 6:00pm, I cultivated my love and passion for nutrition and making healthy recipes. What came of that? Fresh Fit N Healthy, my healthy lifestyle blog and Instagram. What I created out of fun and passion, turned into more than I could have ever asked for or imagined. Once again, God's faithfulness was proven true. I thought I was giving up the greatest opportunity I would get in college by resigning from the cross country team. Yet, in less than a year, God gave me a larger platform to help and inspire people than I ever dreamed of. As an athlete, I was able to reach my team and athletes around me. Now, I was reaching people all over the world. I began receiving emails from young girls and moms alike, both with words of encouragement to continue what I was doing, and stories on how I had helped them. I was speechless. *God, you certainly have a sense of humor. And most importantly, you truly are a good, good Father.*

When we let go of our plans and release the tight grip on the things we hold dearest in life, God has a humorous way of opening doors to better opportunities than we could have ever imagined. It just takes mustering up enough faith in order to take that first step and let go – letting go of that tight grip and releasing your future into His hands. He will never let you down.

Soon enough, I was tested whether or not I would trust Him yet again, when another curveball came my way. T and I, after three and a half years of sharing life together and developing a relationship that we both thought would end in marriage – made the tough decision to let one another go. Unfortunately, when meeting so young, you either grow together or grow apart, and we had grown apart. Despite nothing terrible happening between us, and it truly being one of the most difficult decisions to make, we both knew it was best when we were honest with one another. Once again, my plans fell through. My plans of marrying this incredible guy right out of college and starting a life with him, were shattered, and I was torn apart. For weeks after, I was a wreck; even though I knew deep down that this was what we both needed. At the time, I wasn't sure if it would just be a break for a little time, or it would be the end of us as a couple forever. But I had to trust God that He knew what He was doing, and that He would turn all things, even this heartbreak, into good.

Once again, I can now look back and say that I already see the good. Since that breakup, I have grown in ways that I would never had grown. Even though never thinking I relied on T or was dependent on T for comfort and for security, I realized I actually had been. After the breakup, I realized I no longer had that best friend to run to for things in life – whether good or bad. Instead of running to him in times of despair, or quickly dialing his number to talk to him about something exciting that just happened or something silly I had accidently done, I ran to Jesus. Even though I had girlfriends, T had been my best friend for the last three and a half years; and in losing him, I initially felt alone. It was weird to not have someone to simply go through life with. But it only made me more aware of my need for Jesus. I began living life with Jesus, talking to Him throughout my days – about the bigger, more stressful things and the smaller, more silly things. I came out of this as a better, stronger person, just like I had from all my other past struggles and valleys in life. And yes, we are still friends today and catch up every once in awhile, remaining on the good terms we left off on. He is doing some amazing things himself as he pursues his own passions in this life! He is an incredible guy, and even though no longer a major part of my life, I know will make such an impact in others' lives like he did in mine.

I share these few stories throughout my college years, because they serve as great illustrations for two truths I've come to learn. Just because something is a good thing, does not mean it is the right thing. Running in itself wasn't bad, and it did serve a great purpose in my life for a season. T is a great guy, and I believe our relationship played such a positive role in both of our lives. But there came a time in my life where both running and my relationship with T, were no longer right for my life. Seeking wisdom and discernment in order to distinguish good things versus God things, is key. It is okay to walk away from things (except for in marriage). It doesn't always make you a quitter. It doesn't make you a failure. When it is the healthy choice for you spiritually, physically, or mentally, it makes you wise. Always remember what you deserve. If something no longer serves you, grows you, or makes you happy, it may just be time to walk away from it.

These events also just simply show that life will never be easy. Life will never be picture-perfect; we will never be flawless as human beings – we will mess up. Yet, there is a hope we can always hold on to, no matter the circumstance. We can walk through this inconsistent, imperfect life, knowing we have an unchanging, perfect God walking with us. We can ride this roller-coaster of life, knowing that we can never mess up too much or run too far, to make Jesus leave us or become unavailable to us. And that, my friends, offers us a freedom that no unexpected turn, unanticipated injury, or unpredicted difficulty, can steal. Difficult roads lead to beautiful destinations.

You will mess up. You will make mistakes. You will fall into temptation. You will face difficulties. You will be let down by others. You will experience hurt. You will be thrown curve balls.

But the beautiful thing about those seven sentences above, is that you also have a God that loves you. He loves you so much that even though you may stumble, He will never let you fall. You may mess up, but

He will never abandon you. You may face difficulties, but He will always be right beside you, holding your hand. You may be let down by others, but He never changes and will never disappoint you. You may experience hurt, but He offers you the ultimate comfort and healing. You may be thrown curve balls, but He is ready to jump in front of you and take the hit in order to protect you. Actually, He has already taken the most brutal hit for you, by dying on the cross and rising from the grave. And because of that, He is able to offer us the ultimate gifts – gifts of freedom and of everlasting life.

We may feel frustrated at times when we can't fully understand God or why things happen the way they do, but that is why we are called to live by faith and not by sight. My prayer for you is that you will let go and let God. Let go of the past, and let God take the broken pieces and turn them into something beautiful. Let go of regret, of anger, and of any insecurities, and let God comfort you, fight for you, and strengthen you. Only God can turn your mess into a message, a test into a testimony, a trial into a triumph, and a victim into a victor. And that is exactly what He did for me. My prayer is that this story of mine along with the truths found in God's Word I have shared, will help unlock your prison and give you the keys to the kingdom – providing you a freedom that can never be taken away.

"For they overcame by the blood of the Lamb and by the word of their testimony" (Revelations 12:11, KJV).

This is my testimony.
May it help you overcome and find freedom.

Where is Sarah Grace Spann Now?

Hi, EVERYONE!

First, let me just say *thank you* for your amazing support in purchasing this book. I truly hope it helped you in one way or another! If you post anything about it on social media, I'd love for you to use the hashtag #FreshFitNFREE so I can see you post!

This book ends as I look forward to starting college, including just a few snapshots of my college years. So, here is a little information about what I've been up to since!

During my years at the University of Florida where I earned my undergraduate degree in Food Science and Human Nutrition, I created my healthy-lifestyle blog and Instagram account, Fresh Fit N Healthy, where I share nutritious recipes, health and fitness tips, and my own personal journey. Through Fresh Fit N Healthy, I've been able to travel around the country and work with various health companies, serving as a social-media influencer and athlete. The funny thing is that these opportunities all came from creating an Instagram account just for fun. Talk about Jesus having a sense of humor! I also became a member of Alpha Delta Pi, a sorority in the panhellenic community at the University of Florida, after resigning from running. It was here that I met many of my life-long friends and received an enormous amount of support in all of my dreams I was chasing.

Throughout college, Emily and I became the best of friends, especially when I joined her in becoming a member of Alpha Delta Pi my sophomore year. As for Katie and I, we are extremely close. When recently asked to be in her wedding as a bridesmaid, I was overwhelmed with thankfulness for the complete restoration of our friendship – God is so good. Even though I live in different cities then both Emily and Katie currently, we keep in touch frequently and I know they will be close friends forever.

Which brings me to where life has me at the moment. I'm currently completing both my master's degree in sports nutrition and my dietetic internship at Florida State University in Tallahassee. When I'm not in classes or studying, there are a few places you're bound to find me: my new church I've come to love and help out at, my crossfit gym (yes instead of running I lift heavy now ☺), and in FSU's stadium, volunteering my time with the student athletes. By the summer of 2017, I'll hopefully be a certified registered dietitian! Until then, I'll continue my personal work on the side through Fresh Fit N Healthy and working as a certified personal trainer, as I finish up the dietetic internship program here at Florida State. I may not know what the future holds, but I know who holds my future; and because of that, I can have hope and excitement for what is in store.

Come say hi, and follow my life—along with getting daily inspiration—at the places below:

- Instagram: @freshfitnhealthy
- Blog: www.FreshFitNHealthy.com
- Facebook: Fresh Fit N Healthy
- Twitter: @SarahGraceFFH
- Personal Instagram: @SarahGraceSpann
- #FreshFitNFREE #FreshFitNHealthy
- E-mail: FreshFitNHealthy@gmail.com

Made in the USA
Las Vegas, NV
16 March 2021

19614279R00089